The Strategic Process

10 STEPS FOR PLANNING YOUR INDEPENDENT SCHOOL'S FUTURE

NATIONAL
ASSOCIATION OF
INDEPENDENT
SCHOOLS

ISBN: 1-893021-67-X

Printed in the United States of America.

The National Association of Independent Schools represents approximately 1,300 independent private schools in the United States and other countries. All are accredited, non-discriminatory, nonprofit organizations governed by independent boards of trustees. NAIS's mission is to serve and strengthen member schools and associations by "articulating and promoting high standards of education quality and ethical behavior; to work to preserve their independence to serve the free society from which that independence derives; to advocate broad access for students by affirming the principles of diversity, choice, and opportunity."

To find out more information, go to the NAIS website at *www.nais.org*. To receive a listing of NAIS books, call (800) 793-6701 or (301) 396-5911.

Editor: Sarah Hardesty Bray
Book Design: Fletcher Design, Washington, DC

NATIONAL
ASSOCIATION OF
INDEPENDENT
SCHOOLS

Mixed Sources
Product group from well-managed forests and other controlled sources
www.fsc.org Cert no. SW-COC-2062
© 1996 Forest Stewardship Council

FSC

CONTENTS

Chapter 10
Reassessing and Recalibrating the Plan in Response to Changing Circumstances
The Importance of "Red Flag" Mechanisms
Sustaining Momentum
In Brief:
Key Steps in Implementing and Recalibrating the Plan
Questions to Keep in Mind for Monitoring the Success of Your Plan
Additional Materials:
Inside the Strategy Box — Recalibrating Strategy

SECTION V
Case Histories

SECTION VI
Sample Worksheets

OVERVIEW

By Patrick F. Bassett, NAIS President

Strategic planning as we know it is dead. "Indeed, the whole nature of strategy making — dynamic, irregular, discontinuous, calling for groping, interactive processes with an emphasis on learning and synthesis — compels managers to favor intuition," observes Henry Mintzberg in *The Rise and Fall of Strategic Planning* (Free Press, 1994). "This is probably why all those analytical techniques of planning felt so wrong.... Ultimately, the term 'strategic planning' has proved to be an oxymoron."

A generation ago, the National Association of Independent Schools and its members produced 10-year plans and called the process "long-range planning." By the 1990s, when we were reeling from the aftershocks of hyper-inflation and baby-bust demographics, we realized that a 10-year time frame was unrealistic, so we developed five-year plans and called the process "strategic planning." Well into the first decade of the 21st century, we are realizing that a fixed and inflexible five-year plan also may be unrealistic, as change sometimes comes so dramatically and unexpectedly that the best-laid plans "of mice and men" can be swept away by one tsunami or another.

The publication of this book, *The Strategic Process: 10 Steps for Planning Your Independent School's Future,* is the product of new thinking at NAIS and in the field that favors flexible and nimble "planning" over fixed and rigid "plans." We are moving from "strategic planning" as an isolated event with a fixed, published plan to "strategy-making" and an ongoing "strategic posture," rooted in a five-year vision — one that is based on "data-rich" assessments and trend analysis more then "opinion-rich" thinking.

NAIS believes the entire process of putting together a strategic roadmap can be achieved by a hard-working task force within about six months, with the group or its successor (perhaps the executive committee of the board) reconvening each summer to check the progress down the path, to make recalibrating adjustments as necessary, and to establish the work and goals for the next 12 months. What we are advocating is a new approach:

1. An articulated five-year "vision,"
2. A 12-month "roadmap" to get the journey started, and
3. 24-month and 36-month "sign-posts" and annual "reality checks" to determine whether the signposts are still pointing in the right direction or a "course correction" might be needed.

At the end of three to five years, the full process would start again. While several steps could and may be undertaken simultaneously, there is a new logic for following them in sequential order.

WHY PLAN?

Why should your school adopt a strategic thinking posture and ongoing process? There are three noble and worthwhile purposes and outcomes:

■ **To know objectively how well your school is doing.** Independent schools have been notoriously prone to make opinion-rich decisions based on anecdote and hunch. But current thinking and good management require better decisions that are made after thorough environmental scanning, data mining, and trend analysis. NAIS subscribes to the observation, often attributed to the Nobel-Prize-winning economist George Stigler, that "the plural of anecdote is data." And we are sobered by the observation that Margaret Spellings, the U.S. secretary of education, made to us in her first encounter with private-school representatives: "In God we trust: All others, bring data."

■ **To contribute to a continuing and flexible strategic vision that could result in a new destination and destiny for your school.** In the words of a German proverb: "If you want to give God a laugh, tell Him your future plans." Thus, in the new process, while we still determine the destination that we intend to reach down the road, we recognize that — given the exigencies and unforeseen roadblocks that emerge — detours may happen. So, we reserve the right to adjust course as necessary on the journey to our destination and destiny.

■ **To move your school from "good to great."** A controlling motif of James C. Collins' research and observations in his well-known book of that title (HarperCollins, 2001) is that "good is the enemy of great." How true for independent schools, where change comes slowly, in part, because most often we are good, or at least better than the competition (which in some locales is not a very high standard to beat). Great schools will aim higher, plan strategically to define greatness objectively, not euphemistically or anecdotally, and strategize how to move from "good to great."

NAIS itself has undertaken the new strategy-making process, so we have some idea of what it might look like in schools and a sense of the indicators of a strategy-making posture:

- Frequent staff and constituent data-gathering and environmental scanning;
- Fruitful partnerships, alliances, and joint ventures;
- Ongoing strategic thinking and strategy-driven resource allocation: the development of a venture capital fund;
- Rapid business planning;
- Testing of new ideas, projects, programs;
- Publication of a five-year vision and scenario ("The Vision") with the caveat of staying in a strategy-making posture each year and updating or modifying at an annual strategy meeting the next 12-months' strategic priorities and 24- or 36-month goals as exigencies dictate;
- Restructuring board meetings and the board calendar to create the three levels of trusteeship that Richard P. Chait, William P. Ryan, and Barbara E. Taylor have described in *Governance as Leadership: Reframing the Work of Nonprofit Boards* (John Wiley & Sons, 2004): fiduciary (the ongoing business of the board); strategic (checking on progress and making mid-course corrections for the roadmap), and generative (blue-sky and visionary thinking on what's next).

THE NEW STRATEGIC PLANNING PROCESS

The titles for each of the chapters in this book reflect the stages of this new strategic process:

1. *Setting a Framework for Strategy-Making:* Is your school ready to plan? What process should you use: the traditional strategic plan or the new strategic vision and roadmap? Or a hybrid of the two? What scope of time and scale of effort are you interested in undertaking? How inclusive do you want to be in your planning process?

2. *Planning to Plan:* Can you inspire the board of trustees at the kickstart point? How do you populate the strategic planning task force or com-

mittee with opinion leaders? Where do you begin to undertake the research and reporting out?

3. *Assessing the External Factors that Influence Your School:* What environmental scanning should you do? What can you learn from your own five-year and 10-year trends? From those of NAIS? From your own demographic scanning? From the *NAIS Opinion Leaders Survey: Forecasting Independent School Education to 2025?*

4. *Evaluating Your School's Current Position:* Which tools should you experiment with to do your analysis after you've gathered the data? "SWOT" (strengths, weaknesses, opportunities, threats)? Portfolio Analysis (via value proposition surveying)? War Gaming (a la economist Joseph Schumpeter)? Customers' Customer Analysis©? The Balanced Scorecard? NAIS's workbook, *Financing Sustainable Schools: Six Steps to Re-Engineering Your School's Financial Future?*

5. *Reviewing Your Values and Mission:* Based on your assessment and evaluations, what are your mission (the present, the why you exist) and values (the past and always; the what you believe; the anchoring, resonating essential and enduring tenets for organizations that are "built to last")? How do you organize the constituent and board retreat once you have gathered the facts and developed the scenarios? Following the retreat, how do you test the scenario with larger audiences? Has your environmental scanning and analysis produced a sense that the mission must be enthusiastically affirmed as is, or must it evolve into something different?

6. *Identifying the Key Issues that Confront Your School:* How do you extract and identify your issues? (What are the issues?) Sort them? (How important is each of these?) Evaluate action or inaction on them? (What if you ignore them?) Determine their relationship to mission? (Why do you care about this?) What are your three most insoluble problems?

7. *Creating Your Vision for the Future:* What should your vision be (The future; the what you shall become)? How should you visioncast to visualize the desired and preferred future? Whom will you serve? What skills and values will they need? What do your customers want? What do they need? What should your school be known for in the future that it is not known for now? How do you do the scenario writing and testing?

8. *Determining Goals, Strategies, and Initiatives:* How do you move from goals (the outcomes, the what) to form strategies (the action-oriented approaches, the how) and to articulate initiatives (tactical undertakings

at the departmental levels, the who and when)? How do you backward design the 12-month grid of tasks, timetables, point people (and the parking lot for what, at this point, you think will be the 24-month and 36-month tasks)?

9. *Making Your Strategic Plan Work for You:* How do you live the plan on a daily basis? How do you engage your entire school community in carrying it out? How do you make it work with your operating and financial plans?

10. *Becoming a Strategic-Thinking Organization:* How do you determine when to review the plan and make course corrections? How will you know when your planning has been successful?

The traditional strategic planning process usually started by reaffirming mission and core values, but the process that we've outlined delays that until step five. We do so based on scholarship and experience that suggest the 21st century version of planning should be more "existential," along the lines of what James Ogilvy, a founder of Global Business Network, described in "What Strategists Can Learn from Sartre," in *Strategy + Business* (Winter 2003).That is, rather than assuming your essence or mission is immutable, it may be wise to recognize the existentialist's contrarian perspective that "existence precedes essence."

In other words, the organization evolves as it makes new meaning for itself. It may well be, or perhaps should be, that the new strategic thinking and posture will dictate that everything is on the table — even mission. That all needs to be debated *after* you take a hard look at your own brutal facts — the trends and data, customer satisfaction, and the changing global exigencies that will redefine what it means to be an educated citizen.

THE INDEPENDENT SCHOOL AND THE FUTURE

As each school undertakes the data-gathering, trend-analysis stage, it will develop its own unique assessment of "where we are" and "what we're up against" and "the resources we have to leverage." However, when NAIS conducts its own field-testing of these concepts in the context of Jim Collins' *Good to Great*'s rubric of "brutal facts" vs. "unshakeable beliefs," we have heard back from our constituents "context" themes like the following:

Brutal Facts

(that independent schools must acknowledge and address):

- Competition will increase dramatically for students and teachers in the form of better public schools, charter schools, for-profit schools, home schools, etc.

- Rising costs will alienate current and future customers, make us less affordable and attractive to most of the marketplace, and diminish our diversity. Smaller schools will face survival issues.
- Parents will become more consumer-oriented and difficult to manage.
- Governmental intrusions are likely to increase.
- Resistant cultures will make it more difficult to innovate and lead, and will preclude creative thinking.
- After a massive investment in technology, we are still struggling to capitalize widely upon it to accelerate or customize student learning.
- Prosperity and what Peter Schwartz, in *Inevitable Surprises: Thinking Ahead in a Time of Turbulence* (Gotham, 2004), calls the "long boom" upon which our schools depend may be compromised by global instability, fractious social issues, a larger national deficit, terrorism, and war.
- Ethical relativism will become more pervasive and parenting less effective.
- The weakness, confusion, and underperformance of many school boards will be a huge liability.
- Equity and justice efforts aside, we are still not ready to live in a world where whites are a minority and Christianity is not dominant.

Unshakeable Beliefs
(that schools can leverage to advantage):
- Because of our freedom from government control, independent schools can be mission-driven and child-centered.
- Independent schools have the resources and freedom to innovate in the development and delivery of curriculum and to share that innovation for the betterment of the larger education community.
- Independent schools can make individualized decisions in the best interests of the child and can create diverse, supportive environments where children can thrive.
- Independent schools can continue to survive, even in a tough economy, because of independent financial controls and our focus on high quality and on accountability to the families and communities we serve.
- Independent schools provide an ethos and culture that is values-oriented, one that will always attract and provide value to families.
- Independent schools have three sources of capital that have not even begun to be fully utilized: physical capital, intellectual capital, and social capital.

POSSIBLE STRATEGIC PRIORITIES FOR SCHOOLS

Richard P. Chait, a professor at Harvard University School of Education and a counselor to numerous boards of directors, is fond of paraphrasing an observation made by a nonprofit CEO that "There are three paths to ruin for a head of school: alcohol, the most painful; sexual indiscretion, the most dangerous; and strategic planning, the most certain." This book is intended in part to reassure you and others at independent schools that strategic thinking is an antidote to any apprehension about strategic planning.

Each school at the conclusion of the new process will identify five to eight strategic priorities to achieve its articulated vision of what the school should look like and be five years down the road. From its work in the field, NAIS believes that for many schools, those priorities may include completing some or all of the following conditional statements:

- **Affordability and Accessibility:** "Given that heads identify financing affordable schools that are accessible and diverse as an overarching challenge and that the 10-year NAIS trends indicate continuing pressure on raising tuitions, our school should...."

- **Recruiting, Retaining, Rewarding Talent:** "Given the demographics of an aging workforce near retirement, a generation in college now not attuned to teaching as a career, and concerns about recruitment, retention, and competitive compensation of high-quality faculty, our school should...."

- **Advocacy and Marketing:** Telling the Independent School Story: "Given the increase of proprietary schools, charter schools, home schools, magnet schools, and other types of public and non-public schools as potential competition for the next generation of students, an increase that will require greater advocacy and marketing on behalf of independent schools, our school should...."

- **Communications:** "Given the increasingly demanding nature of parents and the faculty's growing anxiety over the customer, our school should...."

- **Governance:** "Given the continuing outbreaks of volatility in relations between heads and boards in some schools and the lack of growth along Richard Chait's three levels of governance, our school should...."

- **Accountability:** "Given the increased likelihood of media and governmental and parental scrutiny, intrusion, and demands for public accountability, our school should...."

- **Innovation and Change:** "Given the public's perception of independent schools as traditional rather than innovative, and the resistance to change found within independent schools, our school should...."
- **The High-Tech and Global Future:** "Given the 'flat world' imperative for schools to create a curriculum that prepares students for a more techno-logical and global future, our school should...."

Your school, of course, would answer any of these conditional statements, or those you generate on your own, in a way that is uniquely appropriate to your individual circumstances. But if all schools adopt this approach and answer questions like these well, we will surely not only endure but prevail individually and collectively. We also will lead the revolution in American education that is so clearly needed and individually achieve the vision NAIS has for all schools: Schools that are sustainable demographically, environmentally, globally, pro-grammatically, and financially.

February 2007

Starting Off

How often should you plan strategically? Should you always operate within a strategic mindset, or do you need to engage in a specific planning process? Is your school truly ready to think and plan strategically? If so, who should be involved and when?

In the following chapters, Marc T. Frankel and Judith Schechtman, senior consultants and partners with Triangle Associates of St. Louis, MO, describe how you should:

- Assess your school's readiness to plan;

- Determine how often to plan strategically;

- Identify the various roles that the board of trustees, head of school, staff members, and others throughout your school community should play in the planning process;

- Decide whether to use an outside consultant; and

- Establish a plan to plan.

1 SETTING A FRAMEWORK FOR STRATEGY-MAKING

By Marc T. Frankel and Judith L. Schechtman, Senior Consultants and Partners, Triangle Associates

Independent schools that want to plan strategically confront a dilemma: How can you engage in big, deep, and creative thinking about the future when you are hemmed in by a set of immediate operational constraints? It's certainly difficult to think big thoughts when your school is seriously under-enrolled, has experienced multiple years of budget deficits, or, contrariwise, is prospering so much that there is little incentive to change anything. Yet, at the same time, strategies that reflect only incremental, linear progressions will doom your school to be, at best, a market follower and, at worst, on the road to becoming an educational anachronism.

The way to resolve this conflict is to consider a new framework for strategic planning or what we call "strategy-making." This new framework avoids the pressure to formulate both big and small plans at the same time.

PLANNING AS A CONTINUOUS PROCESS

In the traditional process, school boards of trustees have pursued a formal strategic plan every three to five years, resulting in a set of rather rigid goals designed to guide school administrators until the next round of formal planning. But it has become increasingly obvious that the circumstances of real life often change or render meaningless some of the best-crafted formal plans within two or three years. Thus, the new model of successful planning encourages schools to take a *continuous strategy-making posture*. Rather than planning periodically and stopping at that, your independent school should view developing a strategy as a gestalt, a whole with several component parts that taken together equal a strategic posture.

We still recommend that your school engage regularly — but no more frequently than every three years — in a large-scale retreat or workshop to gather input from the widest possible range of stakeholders. In that part of the process, you should encourage creative, big, and generative ideas, and everyone should "think outside of the box." From the workshop will come a gap analysis based on internal and external research — or a gauge of the distance between where the school is and where it aspires to be. From it also will come development of a vision and the establishment of new goals and strategies for the future. Such items, then, could inform a board-level discussion of the continuing viability of the school's mission.

Once your school has adopted a strategic roadmap and destination for five years down the road, then you must keep it relevant and part of the daily life of the institution. Your trustees and administrators should review, recalibrate, and reprioritize school goals at least annually to hone the strategy and ensure the goals' continuing, evergreen nature. As James Dalton, a senior counselor at The Forbes Group, a consulting group in Virginia, has noted in "In Search of Strategy," a paper available on the organization's website, "It's a continuous process, which is what distinguishes it from the traditional three-year plan. Under the pressure of persistent change, real-time strategic thinking replaces much (but not all) of what was formerly provided by intervals of strategic planning. Time condenses under the presence of change to a point where planning and doing run concurrently."

For example, in his book, *Good to Great* (HarperCollins, 2001), James C. Collins suggests that organizations identify the "brutal facts" of their situation —

Some Basic Steps of Strategic Management

■ *Strategic thinking* assesses the future effects of outside forces on the organization. A key component is gathering information and opinions from important constituencies to give planners a solid basis for making decisions.

■ *Strategic planning* creates the school's future based on strategic thinking. It includes developing a vision of the future and identifying what the school needs to do today to achieve that vision.

■ *Strategic implementation* translates the strategic plan into detailed programs and budgets — the work plan of the school — and evaluates them to ensure that they meet students' and others' needs.

■ *Evaluation and feedback* is based on data and reports and determines how closely performance matches the plan.

— *Adapted from The Forbes Group website at* www.forbesgroup.com

undertaking an "environmental scan" of the competitive environment, emerging operational challenges, and unanticipated demands for resources. The board and administration must then confront those facts, yet remain anchored in a set of fundamental and "unshakeable beliefs" about the school and its mission.

We recommend that your board and administration embark on such an exercise every year as a way of meeting new challenges and ensuring that your strategic plan remains fresh and relevant. In that approach, you would scan the environment for emerging issues on a continuing basis. You also could conduct a series of idea-generating sessions each year with key constituency groups in which you evaluate the results of the environmental scan and brainstorm new scenarios for the next 12 months. Based on that process, you can set priorities for the coming year and then place other, less pressing goals back to a 24-month or 36-month parking lot.

In a third part of the strategic planning process, each department or division of your school should use the board-affirmed plan to set its own goals. Once again, if the board adjusts that plan, those departmental and divisional goals should also change. By aligning strategic and annual operating objectives, your planning process can have the collateral benefit of integrating various activities within your school. If that approach is rigorously applied, it means that the upper school won't have a strategic plan that is different from or inconsistent with that of the entire school, or that one campus of a multi-campus system won't work at cross-purposes with the others. In that way, a strategic plan serves to set parameters for your school's various units, while giving each one considerable freedom to determine how to carry out the plan's details.

IS YOUR SCHOOL READY TO PLAN?

Because each independent school's situation is different, there are no absolute ways to determine if your institution is ready to plan strategically. In general, however, certain conditions encourage success.

First, you should be aware of how effective your school's previous planning efforts were, and analyze what did or didn't work in those efforts. If your institution's prior history of planning was somehow negative, it will require extra effort to build credibility and trust among the different groups that have to be energized and contribute to the plan.

Your school should also be prepared to release a tremendous amount of data about itself that it hasn't divulged previously — even through, for example, an accreditation self-study. Market scans, benchmarking, demographic studies, constituent surveys, and trend identification almost always will be essential.

In addition, you must be ready to spend appropriate amounts of money. You will need to pay for the space, food, and other items for the workshop or retreat, plus travel costs to bring out-of-town people to attend. If you plan to conduct research, you will need money for surveys, focus groups, and other studies.

Time resources are equally important. Your school's leaders must be ready to commit to the process, and other members of the school community must be excited about the prospect of their own involvement. Staff members often will need to spend time preparing the details of the retreat and gathering information for the participants. Faculty and staff members' time also will be needed after the workshop for additional meetings and writing sessions. Time must also be allowed for senior administrators to carry out the plan and engage key constituencies, like parents, alumni, and donors. Trustees, too, will need to be involved in making and attending presentations as you roll out the plan. It is not necessary for the entire board to attend every meeting, but each trustee probably should plan to attend at least one or two such sessions during a four-week to eight-week time period.

In *Strategic Planning for Nonprofit Organizations* (second edition, John Wiley & Sons, 2005), Michael Allison and Jude Kaye describe some more intangible, but equally important, conditions for successful planning. They include, among others:

- The commitment, involvement, and support from top leadership;
- A willingness to question the status quo, look at new ways of doing things, ask hard questions, and face difficult choices;
- A commitment to clarifying roles and expectations for all participants in the process, including who will contribute to the plan and make final decisions;
- Good working relationships with no serious conflicts among the players;
- A willingness to gather and use sufficient market research to assess programs and evaluate how to meet needs;
- An adequate commitment of organizational resources to complete the planning process as designed.

Planning Principles and Values

- *Inclusiveness.* Input will be sought from all levels within the organization.

- *Meaningful participation.* Staff members should feel that their participation is substantive, with the potential for real influence on the outcome of the plan; if an individual is expected to implement a strategy, that individual should participate in the shaping of that strategy.

- *Share the work.* The successful completion of the planning process should not depend on one or two people.

- *Focus on the "big picture."* There should be no expectation that every concern or complaint will be addressed by the strategic planning process; however, all critical issues should be addressed, regardless of how difficult those issues may be.

- *Ownership.* We will seek to develop deep ownership of our mission, vision, critical issues, and corporate strategies.

- *Strategy.* Our strategies should be responsive to the environment and based on our understanding of the probable future environment. Much of this understanding will come from in-depth market research.

- *Set benchmarks.* Our strategic plan must be used and results measured against set benchmarks; we must update and renew our planning efforts annually.

— *Michael Allison and Jude Kaye,* Strategic Planning for Nonprofit Organizations *(second edition, John Wiley & Sons, 2005)*
Reprinted with permission of a subsidiary of John Wiley & Sons, Inc.

PRINCIPLES TO GUIDE YOUR SCHOOL'S STRATEGIC PLANNING

We have also identified a number of key assumptions — fundamental ways of looking at the process — that should guide strategic planning. Those assumptions include:

- The meaningful involvement of stakeholders in the planning process is critical to strategy formulation and implementation.

- Support from senior leadership is essential for successful results both during and after the planning process.

- Because values are the basis for organizational decisions, a thorough understanding of the dominant values of the enterprise must drive strategy.

- Constant environmental scanning is essential to understand the factors, both internal and external, that affect the development and usefulness of the plan.

- Throughout the planning process, there should be focus on implementation, with organizational change beginning before the process is completed.

- Most schools require the help of outside expertise to develop a strategic posture and roadmap.

- An effective strategic planning process is dynamic; it is progressive and subject to course corrections as the planning group moves through the process. In a sense, strategic planning is never finished.

IN CONCLUSION

Strategic planning today should be a continuous process. While your school still should consider convening a wide range of constituencies to develop a formal plan about every three years, it also should regularly readjust its goals and how to meet them. Before your school begins to plan, you should be sure that you have the resources to carry out the plan, and that everyone involved in the planning process is ready and willing to follow certain fundamental principles.

Ultimately, the best approach to strategic planning is to think, plan, and act concurrently. You must continually reassess the assumptions on which your strategic plan is based and make small corrections rather than dramatic changes. If you begin the planning process with that overarching framework, you will significantly improve your chances to successfully adapt to the future.

Ideas for Reflection....

What is our reason to plan?

What do we expect will be the benefits?

How would we describe the current state of the institution?

Where are the gaps between the state of the school today and what we want the school to be in three to five years?

— *Christina Drouin, founder and executive director, Center for Strategic Planning, www.planonline.org.*

ADDITIONAL
MATERIALS

Surviving a Revolution of Change

If doing things the old way is dangerous, what is the solution? Since no one has lived through this situation before, answers won't come easily. There are, however, some common-sense principles to guide you, including:

Dump the "This is how we've always done it" syndrome. Look again, from the bottom up, and adjust your school's governance, systems, and programs to the changing realities.

Become future-focused. Get your board to focus not on the minutiae of running the school but on identifying future opportunities and threats and your school's ability to deal with them.

Adopt strategic management. Your leadership needs to have a good idea where the future is leading your school and have the flexibility to adapt to changes as they appear on the horizon. As part of that process, develop an ongoing partnership with all your key constituencies.

Get with the new information technology. It is the driving force of the future. You will not be able to compete without a thorough understanding of its applications.

Think in terms of customers rather than students. Develop niche programs and deliver them to targeted groups of students.

Take an ax to your governance structure. Elaborate governance structures eat up scarce resources and slow down your ability to deal constructively with change. Most committees can be replaced by task forces that disband when their assigned tasks are complete.

Switch from hierarchy to teams. Today the younger people on your staff have been born into this world of rapid change and are often more comfortable with it than your senior people. Empower them to bring you solutions instead of telling them what to do. Learn to be a coach instead of an autocrat.

Resist the temptation to cut staff. After a wave of downsizing, many in the corporate world now find themselves bereft of some of their most experienced and talented people — and with little improvement in the bottom line. While you should always terminate incompetent people who threaten your school's success, keep those who clearly contribute and are willing to adapt to the new realities.

— Adapted from The Forbes Group website at **www.forbesgroup.com**

THE STRATEGIC PROCESS

Strategic Planning Terminology

People come to strategic planning in independent schools from many different backgrounds, so disagreement on the basic definitions of planning terms will probably arise. A common language enables everyone to participate with clarity and understanding. While the words below and their definitions can serve as a guide, you may use other terms or you may select similar terms and give them different meanings. Whatever your choice, agree on a common glossary early in your process.

Core Values

Core values are those three to five essential ideals that define your school and to what it ascribes worth above all else. Core values answer the question *"What do we stand for?"*

Mission

Mission is a broad description of your school's purpose. Mission answers the question *"Why do we exist?"*

Strategic Issues

Strategic issues are the highest priority challenges facing your school based on the results of the research and analysis phase of your planning process. Your strategic plan addresses and resolves these strategic issues. Strategic issues answer the question *"What are the strategic imperatives that we must address over the next three to five years?"*

Vision

A vision is a word picture of what success looks like for your school at an appointed time in the future (typically three to five years). Your vision statement will provide direction and inspiration for goal-setting and will be a shared view of the future. Vision answers the question *"What does success look like for us at the appointed time in the future?"*

Goals

Goals are broad statements of what must be achieved in order to reach your vision. Goals must be clear and understandable. Typically, four to six overarching goals define the major work that will lead to realization of vision. Goals answer the question *"What must we accomplish in order to actualize our vision?"*

Strategies

Strategies outline major steps for attaining overarching goals. Typically, four to six strategies can be crafted to define the directional approaches required to fulfill each overarching goal. Strategies answer the question *"How will we achieve our goals?"*

Initiatives

Initiatives are the projects, programs, and activities that are identified as necessary to achieve a goal. Initiatives are the tactical implementation of strategy and answer the question *"What specific projects, programs, and activities will operationalize our strategies and lead us to reach our goals?"*

Performance Outcomes

Performance outcomes are measurable statements of results expressing the way a goal or initiative will positively impact the attitude, awareness, knowledge, skills, behavior, status, and/or condition of a specific individual or group. Performance outcomes answer the question *"What is the evidence of success?"*

— *Christina Drouin, founder and executive director, Center for Strategic Planning,* www.planonline.org

2 PLANNING TO PLAN

By Marc T. Frankel and Judith L. Schechtman, Senior Consultants and Partners, Triangle Associates

The first step in a strategic planning process is when a board of trustees commissions the development of a plan based on a specific need, issue, or purpose. Whatever that is, the next step involves how your school should set parameters on what it wants to accomplish though the planning process. Are there levels of strategic planning that are appropriate for different times of your institution's history or at different stages of its strategic development? Should institutions with different resources plan in different ways?

Several factors will affect how broad or narrow the planning scope should be, including the effectiveness of your school's previous strategic plans, its current financial status, and the state of your board and administrative leadership. What is important is that you should articulate the planning scope clearly and in advance so that everyone involved in the process is aware of how to move forward.

In their excellent book, *Strategic Planning for Nonprofit Organizations* (second edition, John Wiley & Sons, 2005), Michael Allison and Jude Kaye suggest three types of planning approaches: abbreviated, moderate, and extensive. The abbreviated format may be just a one-day retreat from which a short planning document of only a couple of pages is developed. At the other extreme, you may select an extensive planning process that encompasses numerous workshops, meetings, and a lengthy written document, and that lasts as long as nine months. You may seek a middle, moderate ground and organize several days of major workshops, followed by various smaller, follow-up meetings over the course of several months, and the publication of a mid-sized document.

Your school's specific reasons for planning will significantly influence the way you should approach planning, and who should participate on the strategic planning team. When your school is thinking about embarking on a strategic planning process, it is often facing some important issues:

- Should we buy a building or expand the one we have?
- If we embark on a major fund-raising campaign, what do we hope to accomplish?
- How do we deal with major new competition for students from another educational institution?

Christina Drouin, founder and executive director of the Center for Strategic Planning, notes that "a small K-6 independent school in an enrollment crisis will benefit more from a compact, sonar-like planning approach than a K-12 urban, day-boarding school looking down the line at a capital campaign." Similarly, a K-12 school with no experience in strategic planning might adopt a simpler, less holistic model than a school of comparable size and complexity approaching its fifth planning cycle. Each school is different and must select the approach that is best for it.

Key Questions to Ask in Getting Started

- Who will make up the core planning team?

- What do governance (the board) and management (the head and administrative leadership team) see as the school's strategic issues?

- What planning horizon will you use? Will this be a three-year or a five-year plan?

- How long will you engage in the planning process? Will you devote six months, nine months, or a full academic year?

- What planning model will you use? Will it be inclusive? How much research will it involve? Will it be grounded in core values and mission? Will the plan include general concepts through the tactical elements? Or will the plan fly at 30,000 feet and include only vision, goals, and strategies? Will you even have a vision, or will goals and strategies alone form the basis of your plan?

- What structures and processes are already in place to help you organize this planning process?

- Whose authorization will be required at what points in the process?

- Will you use an outside facilitator?

- Who comes to mind as possessing one or more of the attributes helpful to a strategic planning team?

- To whom will the strategic planning team be accountable?

— *Christina Drouin, founder and executive director, Center for Strategic Planning,*
  www.planonline.org.

THE ROLES OF YOUR SCHOOL'S TRUSTEES, HEAD, AND STAFF

The etymological root of *to govern* is *to steer.* Your board of directors should steer the planning process and participate in the strategic planning workshop. Your trustees are the guardians of your school's overarching and long-term goals, and they should lead your staff in setting the institution's top priorities.

Whatever your trustees' direct involvement in the strategic plan is, they need to be kept up-to-date throughout the planning process. In addition, the board must ensure that the plan is fresh — that it continues to meet the school's needs by taking into account emerging strategic issues. Trustees should revisit the plan during at least one board meeting each year, modifying the strategic priorities for the next 12, 24, or 36 months, as exigencies dictate.

A steering committee or task force of the board can be useful in helping your school develop appropriate parameters for planning. Some boards have a standing strategic planning committee. The steering committee acts on behalf of the governing board to frame and launch the planning project in a way that equips it for success.

Typically, the steering committee or task force will need to meet only a few times; its role is to set the broad parameters for the plan. It will review any previous strategic plans, the results of those plans, and how effective they were. It will set the planning framework, the beginning and ending dates of the process, and the methodology that your school will use in planning. The committee also will identify the state of the institution and the key issues that the plan should address, if an outside consultant will be hired, and who in your school's community should serve on the strategic planning team. It should also commission the team to begin work on the plan, as well as establish the expected reporting relationship between itself and the team.

Although strategic planning is a key responsibility of the board of trustees, it often is the head of school who initiates the process. He or she should help guide and inform the development of your plan and be the driving force in carrying it out. Strategic planning consultant Christina Drouin has said, "While the ultimate responsibility of the achievement of the plan's vision rests with the governing board, the plan relies for its momentum on the active participation and support of the head of school as chief ambassador and vision-bearer." Your head should be a member, ex officio or regular, of the planning task force or subcommittee.

Staff members may sit on ad hoc committees with members of the board or within the school community and are key sources of data and information about the school. They should be involved in identifying current and future needs and be able to assess the key internal and external forces that influence your school's operations. Your school head also may assign to various staff members some specific responsibilities for developing and carrying out the plan.

SELECTING YOUR STRATEGY-AND-DESIGN TASK FORCE

The members of your planning team can be administrators, faculty members, trustees, parents, alumni, students, donors, and others. It often is best to have between six and 12 people on the team, including the head of school, at least one trustee, and the person responsible for writing the final plan. Although you can make your planning team larger if you want to be more inclusive, you don't want it to be so large that it is hard to get things accomplished.

You should carefully select the members so they bring a variety of attributes and skills — big-picture thinking, research expertise, analytical ability — to the task at hand. The team should be a diverse group of stakeholders in the school and include people who are visionary as well as those who can get those visions accomplished. In addition, the group should have credibility and respect with other people throughout your school's community; they should be the opinion leaders, or what Malcolm Gladwell in *The Tipping Point* (Little, Brown and Company, 2000) calls the "mavens" and "connectors."

The team's first assignment will be to determine who will do what within the team, how decisions will be made, and how often it will meet. It also should outline in detail the planning process and timeline, including key dates on which certain planning objectives should be accomplished. It should start to evaluate the major issues confronting your school and begin to identify possible benchmarks and ways to measure planning results. It also should determine the data that will be needed — for example, statistics on the characteristics of your student body, financial trends over the past three years, lists of competitors — as well as how it will be collected, and who will collect it. In short, it should develop a plan to plan.

ENGAGING OTHER PEOPLE IN THE PROCESS

The entire campus community should be involved and engaged in some way in the strategic plan and understand how the process will unfold. Thus, one of the first and most important jobs is to announce formally the new planning

Characteristics to Consider in Potential Members of the Planning Team

- A knowledge of and commitment to the school;

- Open-mindedness;

- The inclination to listen to others;

- Tolerance for some ambiguity;

- The ability to work comfortably within a group process;

- An understanding of the role of questioning and consensus;

- The willingness to commit the time required of team members to participate fully.

— *Susan C. Stone,* Shaping Strategy *(NAIS, 1993)*

process and to alert representatives of all key school groups that they will be asked to participate at various times. Those groups might include students, parents, grandparents, trustees, faculty members, administrators, alumni, donors, members of the community, and perhaps representatives of nearby independent schools.

If you are as inclusive as possible, you will gain enthusiasm and buy-in from the people who often will carry out the plan. You also will obtain a broader range of insights and ideas for the plan that help you to make more informed decisions. You even may inspire greater allegiance among the important constituencies of your school in general.

"By intentionally involving in the plan's formation all the constituencies who will have responsibility for its execution, a school affirms in a meaningful way the importance of every individual in creating the desired future state," Christina Drouin has observed. "Processes that involve multiple opportunities for constituency opinion and information gathering — focus groups, surveys, one-on-one interviews, strategic-thinking sessions, scenario development, and all-day planning symposia or community visioning days to which everyone is invited — establish a new threshold for cooperation and shared responsibility and pave the way for accountability during implementation."

As part of this effort, you should create a communications plan that outlines who should receive certain information and when. One of the first communications probably should be a personal letter from the head of your school to all relevant stakeholders. You also might consider other tools, such as an article in your school's periodical, information on your school's website, and presentations at alumni and donor events. You want to ensure that people throughout the school community are aware of the plan's purpose, how they will participate in the strategic planning process, and what you hope the outcome of that process will be.

SHOULD YOU USE AN OUTSIDE CONSULTANT?

When a school can afford the expense, an outside consultant can be very helpful to lead a planning workshop or retreat and guide the writing of any planning document. Because consultants have no stake in the specific outcomes of the strategic planning process, they often are in a better position to identify the hard facts, encourage and bring together disparate viewpoints, and find a way to build bridges across differences among people. A good consultant also brings experiences with similar schools and an awareness of independent school trends that can add significant value to the conversation. In addition, you can use a consultant as another set of hands to perform a wide variety of planning tasks.

In many instances, a board and administrative team may be comfortable recalibrating your strategy without external help. At other times, you may need a consultant to keep the process on track. The school's trusteeship committee may be in the best position to gauge the maturity level of the board and its readiness to shoulder the work alone between large-scale workshops — the kind that happen every three to five years — where multiple stakeholders are invited to spend a day or two participating in the planning process.

To use consultants effectively, you should know why you are hiring them, what you expect from them, and how they are going to deliver it. You should select an experienced consultant who listens from the start. Communicate clearly with him or her about your school's situation and needs. You also should be willing to let the consultant guide the process and not get in his or her way, as well as to provide information and access to people and data, so the consultant can learn the most about your school and its environment.

Stephen C. Carey, the author of *The Association and Nonprofit Strategic Planning and Research Guide* and the president of Association Management and Marketing Resources, strongly recommends that organizations not try to "go it alone" or use staff members as facilitators because of the perceptions and prejudices they might bring to the task. He suggests selecting an experienced facilitator based on the following criteria, among others:

- Formal training in facilitative skills;

Tips for Hiring Consultants

■ You may choose to have different consultants…. For example, you may hire one consultant to facilitate the planning process and another to do some research.

■ Interview at least two consultants. You will be able to explore different approaches to the project and may utilize the ideas of more than one consultant.

■ For substantial projects, ask for references and a written price bid from each consultant interviewed.

■ Agree on one person to whom the consultant will report. The process will get confusing if different people are asking for different things.

■ Have a written memorandum of understanding or contract with the consultant, with payments based on the consultant's performance of agreed-on tasks.

■ Throughout the project, give the consultant feedback on his or her work.

■ If the organization is working with other consultants, make sure the other consultants and the planning consultants are informed of each others' work and coordinating each others' efforts.

■ Do not expect a consultant to make tough decisions or value-based choices for you. A consultant can help articulate alternative courses of action and the implications of various choices, but the organization's decision-makers should make the important decisions.

■ Agree in advance how you will pay the consultant's fees, including any overruns.

— *Michael Allison and Jude Kaye,* Strategic Planning for Nonprofit Organizations *(second edition, John Wiley & Sons, 2005)*

■ Formal training in qualitative and quantitative market research techniques and designs;

■ Previous experience in facilitating strategic planning assignments; and

■ Experience in the governance, administration, financial, marketing, and communications areas of the organization.

Even though your consultant can play a crucial role, you should not expect him or her to make the final decisions for you. That is the responsibility of the school's top leaders.

SITUATIONS TO AVOID

It's important to get your planning process off to the right start. In our experience, the key issues that can derail schools include:

- A lack of inclusiveness — for example, not getting a broad enough swath of stakeholders engaged in the process;
- Parsimony — for example, minimizing costs and/or time by relying on insufficient or incorrect data or by trying to develop a plan without external help;
- A short-term problem-solving focus — for example, only dealing with issues of immediate concern rather than those of long-term impact, like how to repair a roof rather than what physical plant needs are suggested by demographic shifts in the local population;
- Agenda hijacking — or allowing the pet interests of one or two people, regardless of how influential, to drive the plan.

WHAT DO YOU WANT YOUR PLAN TO ACCOMPLISH?

Where do you hope your school will be at the end of the process? You should begin with a clear sense of the answer to that question, because what you hope to accomplish will determine how you develop the strategic plan. You should evaluate your reason for planning. Is it to increase revenues for operational solvency, add or eliminate a boarding component to a day school to address demographic realities, embark on a new capital campaign to fund faculty compensation competitively, or develop a 21st-century vision and program? Your board, top administrators, and planning team should identify the specific questions and choices that you hope the planning process will enable you to confront *before* you try to determine the answers. Formulating the general issues in advance will help you apply strategic planning tools efficiently and effectively.

IN CONCLUSION

Every school must determine how extensive the planning process should be and who should be involved in it. Many institutions establish a steering committee or task force of the board to develop a plan to plan. The strategic planning process should be overseen by the board, but the head of the school should take primary responsibility for the plan and its success. You should establish a planning committee to manage the key details of the process, which should include communicating about and involving a wide range of people in the plan. Where possible, it often is good to engage an outside consultant to help lead a strategic planning retreat and other aspects of the plan. Effectively planning to plan in the initial stages of developing your strategy will set you on a focused course toward reaching your goals successfully.

ADDITIONAL
MATERIALS

How the School Head Can Keep Institutional Strategic Planning on Track

Before a New Planning Process

- Test the board of trustees for strategic planning readiness and commitment.
- Prepare the board for an inclusive process in which it has a critical role.
- Involve the board in the strategic planning and thinking processes.
- Determine the state of the school and the type of planning required (for example, first plan, crisis, or comprehensive).
- Determine the planning parameters, including budget and timeline.
- Determine if outside help is needed; if yes, select a facilitator.
- Understand the principles of strategic planning and strategic thinking.
- Consider how the re-accreditation cycle and strategic planning cycle can be coordinated to form one rather than two operating systems.

During

- Guide the process and maintain a visual presence.
- Encourage and recognize constituent participation.
- Provide staff support.
- Serve as a key guardian of institutional identity; make certain that all decisions pass through the dual filter of core values and mission.
- Champion strategic planning and strategic thinking.
- Advocate for the plan's adoption by the board of trustees.

After

- Serve as the lead vision-bearer.
- Identify and act on strategies to get the plan off the shelf and into action, including the development of a prioritizing, tracking, and monitoring system.
- Allocate resources to implementation including time, money, and support.
- Surface and overcome barriers to plan implementation; facilitate progress.
- Set annual goals, including the head's goals, based on the vision and goals of the plan.
- Hold people accountable for results.
- Recognize and reward achievements.
- Communicate progress widely and often using a variety of media and formats.
- Encourage feedback loops and ongoing evaluation.

■ Create a climate of strategic thinking where open inquiry is the norm, assumptions undergo continuous testing, and plans are adaptable to change.

— Christina Drouin, founder and executive director, Center for Strategic Planning, www.planonline.org.

Determining Where You Are Today

Before you can plan for the future, you must determine where your school is today. In the next two chapters, Bruce Butterfield, president of The Forbes Group, a consulting firm in Vienna, VA, describes how to:

- Evaluate and take stock of your current operations;

- Define the key questions you need to ask yourself about the environment in which you will be operating in the future; and

- Identify the information that your school needs to gather to plan effectively.

Section II

3 ASSESSING THE EXTERNAL FACTORS THAT INFLUENCE YOUR SCHOOL

By Bruce Butterfield, President, The Forbes Group

Most organizations tend to view the future through the lens of the present or even the past. The danger is that the past is not necessarily prologue.

There are risks in projecting today onto tomorrow, no matter how thoughtfully it is done. The tendency is to assume that principles long accepted as true remain true, and that the future runs in a straight line from the present. If we had taken that approach in 2001, the World Trade Center towers would still stand. If we had done that in 1994, the word "Internet" would not be in our vocabulary. If we had made that assumption 20 years ago, the Soviet Union and the Berlin Wall would still exist.

Still, clues to the future often do reside in the present. When management guru Peter Drucker was asked how he did such a good job of forecasting, he replied, "I don't forecast. I identify what is visible but not yet seen."

THE FORESIGHT MODEL OF FUTURE ANALYSIS

The Institute for Crisis Management, which tracks 16 categories of crisis events through news reports, says that in 2003, 71 percent of crises were smoldering. In other words, they were visible but not yet in full view. So how do you spot them?

Some of the characteristics of tomorrow are observable today. For example:

■ The young, middle-aged, and elderly of the next decade already are here. They can be studied, and projections of their behavior can be made from current data. Educational institutions like independent schools are particularly well poised to analyze the future demographically, because they already are dealing with the next generation in their classrooms.

The Five Keys to Sustainability in the 21st Century

- *Financial sustainability:* becoming more efficient and less costly;

- *Environmental sustainability:* becoming more green and less wasteful;

- *Global sustainability:* becoming more networked internationally and less parochial in outlook;

- *Programmatic sustainability:* becoming more focused on the skills and values that the 21st-century marketplace will seek and reward, and less narrowly isolated in a traditional disciplines approach to teaching and learning;

- *Demographic sustainability:* becoming more inclusive and representative of the school-aged population and less unapproachable financially and socially.

— NAIS Opinion Leaders Survey: Forecasting Independent Education to 2025 *(NAIS, 2005)*

- Public policy decisions that drive worldwide economic trends take years to change direction, so current economic indicators can provide us with a glimpse of the economy in the second decade of the 21st century.

- Political trends are in place that will determine the shape of government for many years. These include terrorism, the emergence of China, protests about globalization, and the response to corporate misbehavior, to name a few.

- Emerging technologies can be extrapolated into new products and services, and new questions can be explored: What is the future of video gaming in education? How will migration of the Web to cell phones affect research and learning?

So, how do you sort out these things? You need to ask a few key questions in order to avoid being blindsided by the future. Those questions include:

- What is the future you most fear?
- What is the future you most desire?
- Where are the clues in what you know about the future?
- What will happen if you stay on your present course?
- Will you like that outcome?

One of the best ways to answer those questions is to use the foresight model of futures analysis. Foresight is a process that requires futures-focused thinking. It looks at long-range options and considers possible alternative futures that may confront an organization. Futures-focused thinking helps articulate goals within the framework of a vision that describes the future the organization most wants to create. Foresight and futures thinking include five primary activities:

1. identifying and monitoring change,
2. considering and critiquing the impacts of change,
3. imagining alternative possible futures,
4. visioning preferred futures, and
5. planning, team building, and implementing desired change.

Those five foresight activities are interrelated as data and actions flow from one to the next. They are most effective when performed in concert, progressively and continuously. Future thinking and strategic planning are a process rather than events, and they lead to creating implementation plans and methods for evaluating an institution's progress in order to keep the process moving forward. The first two activities of the foresight model are presented here; the final three will be covered in later chapters.

IDENTIFYING AND MONITORING CHANGE

Foresight begins with the identification, and subsequent monitoring of, changing trends. As a first step, your school needs to assess patterns of change that have influenced it in the past, as well as to collect baseline data on conditions that are influencing its operations today and may influence them in the future. Such efforts will provide a context within which the school can identify ongoing cycles, recurrent trends, or emerging new issues such as technological innovations or fundamental value shifts among key school constituencies.

How can your school find those areas of potential change lurking just under the surface? It's easier than you may think, but it involves commitment from staff and leaders to keep up with the information. Two of the most successful tools that you can use to identify and monitor change are environmental scanning and economic analysis. These involve identifying possible future scenarios that pose threats and opportunities for the school, and recognizing the school's strengths and weaknesses in order to address them. The environmental scan offers a valuable opportunity to seek the views of all the school's key opinion groups and to start building a consensus among them. Scanning is an essential part of strategic thinking; it prevents organizations from being blindsided.

Most environmental scans are extremely flawed, because they are internally focused and treated as an event rather than as a continuous process. Scanning is like the searchlight on a riverboat, which constantly is sweeping the darkness to identify sandbars, debris, and the open channel. The sweep needs to be from shore-to-shore and as far into the distance as it is possible to see with precision. There is a limit to how far you can see ahead, so scans that look out 20 to 30 years are more subject to error than those that look out five to 10 years.

An environmental scan may address four different areas of change, including:

- Cycles or changes that occur over an observable time period and are rather predictable (for example, seasons and weather patterns).

- Trends or changes that move in a direction over time. Trends are not new — a lot of data and information about them exists, and they have been observed for a period of time (for example, global warming, population changes, etc.).

- Wildcard events or sudden, discontinuous change that is unexpected and unpredictable (for example, the fall of the Berlin Wall, the September 11 tragedies).

- Emerging issues or seeds of changes that will initiate a trend over time. That is the type of change that most interests futurists. If you are able to sniff out an emerging issue, you have the potential for real leverage in how that issue eventually affects your institution.

When scanning the environment, you should be concerned about "micro" trends that immediately affect your school — such as how many students in your neighborhood apply each year. You also should consider broader trends that impact society at large. To ensure that all possible sources of change are considered, it is important that the school take a 360-degree view and monitor changes in five crucial systems, which are represented by the acronym "STEEP." These are:

Societal/individual systems

Technological systems

Economic systems

Environmental/natural systems

Political/regulatory systems

Changes in each system in the macro environment will affect the working environment of the institution and any decisions and actions taken with regard to the critical issues facing it.

Christina Drouin, the founder and executive director of the Center for Strategic Planning, has suggested that some of the strategic information that an independent school might seek in a STEEP analysis includes:

- Trends in geo- and psycho-demographics (the distribution of population by socioeconomics, race, income, educational attainment, and lifestyle looked at geographically by market area);
- Trends and issues in multiculturalism and diversity;
- Changes in public opinion in the areas of values and ethics;
- Educational trends and issues in public and private K-12 education;
- Educational trends and issues in higher education; and
- Competitive market analysis based on peer review.

A thorough STEEP analysis involves scanning articles, publications, journals, websites, and other sources for tidbits of particularly interesting information in the five categories that could have real potential for creating change.

STEEP Questions for Independent Schools

How might STEEP (social, technological, economic, environmental, and political) factors play out in your school setting? Considering the broad categories of student and faculty retention and recruitment, affordability, educational program, and facilities — strategic considerations that most schools have in common — below is a sample set of questions that tie external STEEP factors to an independent school setting. You can explore them with any constituency group through various venues, such as interviews, focus groups, online conversations or surveys, and strategic-thinking sessions.

- How might college and university needs for and expectations of independent school graduates evolve over time?

- How might the overall external environment in which the school operates evolve over time?

- How can the school sustain or improve its ability to attract outstanding students and families aligned with its values and mission?

- What will be required from the formal training and educational processes to provide an optimal experience for all students?

- How must the curriculum evolve to provide students with the level of education needed to meet the demands of the 21st century?

- How can the school's value proposition meet changing consumer needs and expectations today and in the future? Where are the gaps?

— *Christina Drouin, founder and executive director, Center for Strategic Planning (adapted from the U.S. Naval Academy strategic plan, "Key Issues for the 21st Century"), www.planonline.org.*

NAIS AS A STEEP RESOURCE

Such scanning is a labor-intensive process that can be difficult for over-taxed staff and part-time volunteers to perform well. Yet, the more sources of information that you scan, the richer the scan and the greater the likelihood of correctly identifying emerging issues and trends that could affect the school. Moreover, scanning should not be considered a one-shot deal. You should be assessing trends in your external environment on a continuing basis.

To help you, NAIS has collected a wealth of STEEP information: backgrounders, position papers, and statistics that are available online, as well as books and articles in *Independent School* magazine on strategic issues.

■ NAIS surveyed a number of opinion leaders in education, business, and media, and asked them to predict trends that will impact education over the next two decades. The association also asked them to suggest action steps for schools to take to prepare and position themselves for those trends. NAIS produced a report, the *NAIS Opinion Leaders Survey: Forecasting Independent Education to 2025,* which summarized the responses and provided supplementary research in five areas: demographics, social forces, economic trends, the political climate, and science and technology.

■ In the foreword to NAIS's eighth edition of Mary Hundey DeKuyper's popular *Trustee Handbook,* NAIS president Patrick F. Bassett cites the six strategic issues that NAIS survey research has identified as top-priority challenges for schools:

1. Recruiting, retaining, and competitively compensating high-quality faculty;
2. Financing the school;
3. Managing technology;
4. Developing the 21st century curriculum;
5. Communicating to internal and external audiences;
6. Creating more diverse and inclusive communities.

■ In *Marketing Independent Schools in the 21st Century,* edited by Catherine O'Neill Grace (NAIS, 2001), Mark Mitchell discusses several STEEP factors specifically related to tuition and school costs in the chapter "Tackling the Affordability Dilemma." He sets forth four critical challenges to schools: the minority majority, increasing income inequality, the evolving household, and the escalation in tuition and pricing. He challenges schools to find new ways to think about how they market themselves, and how they invest in achieving their missions through financial-aid programs and other forms of tuition assistance. Mitchell also highlights the concepts of prestige, affordability, value, and sacrifice (PAVS) to help schools understand public perceptions of school prices.

■ NAIS underwrote a public opinion poll in 1999, conducted by Jeffrey T. Wack, professor at Yale University and head of JT Wack & Company, a strategic marketing consulting practice in New Haven, CT. Among its findings were the following five features seen by the public as essential to a quality school:

1. employing high quality teachers;
2. preventing drug and alcohol use;
3. keeping students motivated and enthusiastic about learning;
4. challenging students to do their best; and
5. encouraging parents to participate in their child's education.

■ The NAIS publication, *Financing Sustainable Schools — Six Steps to Re-Engineering Your School's Financial Future,* offers schools a rubric for assessing their own trends that impact budget, benchmarking them against comparable schools, developing metrics (data proxies) for measuring success, and using the NAIS Online Financial Calculator to project alternative and preferred financial futures.

■ NAIS Demographics Center: As a way to help school leaders keep up with major changes taking place in the demographic makeup of their local, state, and regional areas, NAIS has partnered with Easy Analytic Software, Inc. (EASI) to establish an online service to provide members with demographic data. The NAIS Demographic Center offers two types of reports. The Basic Reports for Independent Schools include demographic variables that have been especially selected for their relevance in the decision-making process for independent school administrators, whereas the Additional Reports for Advanced Use contain demographic variables in general that can provide a more sophisticated analysis of the demographic changes in the American landscape. By running these reports, you can assess how these variables have changed over time and will continue to change, and compare them with the demographics of your own school. By knowing these data, you can make strategic decisions that will ensure that your school survives and thrives in an ever-changing marketplace. Watch *www.nais.org* for details about the Center.

■ NAIS Independent School Survey Builder: One way to capture data relevant to your institutions is to use the NAIS Parent Satisfaction Survey, Alumni Survey, and Climate Survey, which NAIS will offer through the Independent School Survey Builder, to be launched in Spring 2007. Watch *www.nais.org* for details.

CONSIDERING AND CRITIQUING THE IMPACTS OF CHANGE

Once the task force has gathered lots of great information, your school is ready for the next step. Your school needs to assess the effects that cascade from ongoing change throughout the macro environment, and also evaluate what impact those effects may have on the institution. How will this change influence the school's day-to-day activities? Who has been newly advantaged or disadvantaged by the advent of this change? What trade-offs might you face?

One way to critique and consider impacts of change is to benchmark another industry or profession, so you can study how they were affected by similar changes in their environment. Benchmarking or peer review is a powerful tool to learn what was successful and unsuccessful in other organizations in terms of how they dealt with changes in the macro environment. It helps you discover how schools similar to yours operate, deal with problems and issues, and plan ahead. The aim is to evaluate where your institution is currently positioned as the basis for determining where you would like to go in the future.

How should you select the best institutions to study? The criteria might be similar mission, location, size, budget, endowment, or other qualifications. NAIS can provide support — through such programs as StatsOnline, a database of various statistics about independent schools — in helping you select schools for benchmarking your progress.

Another common tool is cross-impact analysis, which measures the correlation between certain variables. It identifies how developments in one STEEP area will affect those in another, the strength of that influence, and whether it makes a specific outcome more or less likely. The major benefit of using cross-impact analysis is the ability to show how one situation changes another. It involves working with a matrix to establish causality variables and analyzing each pair of variables for the degree of impact (high, medium, low) and the direction of that impact (positive or negative).

For example, if you discover that Congress may pass a new law that would affect the tax treatment of donated goods and services, it would be prudent to understand how that might influence your fund-raising efforts. Cross-impact analysis is an efficient, quantitative way to see such connections.

THE FUTURING WHEEL

This technique is used primarily in brainstorming sessions. A small group produces a list of future possibilities based on the scanning data. The group then eliminates those that are highly unlikely or too similar to the present. The remaining items are developed into three to six subtopics. Those subtopics are divided into three to six more topics. The idea is to identify the related areas and assess potential impact. This method is not as widely used as cross-impact analysis, but it is an effective qualitative way to identify problems and related events.

IN CONCLUSION

One of the first steps in strategic planning is to discern the external forces that are influencing your school now and will influence it in the days and years ahead. Some of those forces will be readily apparent, while others will require foresight and analysis. That includes identifying and monitoring change, and then critiquing the impacts of various types of changes. You must take a broad view and evaluate changes in society, technology, the economy, the environment, and the political system. While it can be time-consuming, such scanning is critical to strategic thinking and will help your school avoid being blindsided by the future.

ADDITIONAL
MATERIALS

Online External Scanning Resources

American Demographics, The Futurist (published by the World Future Society), and *Revolution: Business and Marketing in the Digital Economy* are just a few of the magazines with current and useful summaries of the prevailing demographic trends. They provide an overview of issues, trends, and forecasts in a host of areas. However, the Worldwide Web provides the fastest, most cost- effective, and easiest means of searching for specific demographic data. Provided below are excellent demographic websites:

The U.S. Census Bureau
www.census.gov

A well-designed site with a remarkable array of data. Includes a variety of demographic projections. Relatively user-friendly if you have the right software already loaded.

Fed Stats
www.fedstats.gov

All of the public statistics from over 100 public agencies. If the government keeps the statistic and makes it public, you can find it on this site! Similar to the U. S. Census site, yet even more data, however, less user-friendly.

"The Right Site®"Easi Demographics
www.easidemographics.com

Strong selection of reports detailing family incomes, race, property ownership, etc. Searchable by state, city, zipcode, or even down to the neighborhood level using specific latitude and longitude. Great site, particularly for beginners!

American Demographics Magazine
http://adage.com/americandemographics/

Many of the magazine's great articles are available.

EconData
www.econdata.net

Links to nearly every government and academic data source imaginable. Has the best "top 10" links list anywhere. For highly detailed economic research, this site might be the place to start.

Economic Information Systems
www.econ-line.com

Great site for economic data. Very user-friendly with terrific graphs and graphics.

GeoStat: Geospatial & Statistical Data Center
University of Virginia Library
http://fisher.lib.virginia.edu/

Incredibly detailed data, searchable in nearly every manner you can imagine. This is a great site for highly specific research, but not for the rookie researcher or technology novice.

Premier Insights
www.premierinsights.com

Some great national data free, and will send other reports by e-mail or by fax.

— Adapted from a 1999 listing by D. Scott Looney, now head of Hawken School (Ohio).

assure
FUTURE
INSTITUTIONAL
relevance

4 EVALUATING YOUR SCHOOL'S CURRENT POSITION

By Bruce Butterfield, President, The Forbes Group

The goal of the next step in the strategic planning process is to evaluate the effectiveness of your school's current programs and services in meeting the needs of its constituents, including faculty, staff and administration, students and parents, alumni, parents of alumni, and grandparents. In today's brutally competitive environment, there are no more fences around turf. Independent schools are in a struggle for students, faculty, resources, and recognition. Of primary concern is how institutions stack up against their competition.

Which services and activities make the most difference to you and your key audiences? Which do you need to grow aggressively, and which to change significantly? What are your school's core competencies, or its distinct competitive advantages?

TRADITIONAL METHODS FOR ASSESSING YOUR SCHOOL

There are many tools to help you gather and analyze information about the strength of your institution's various internal operations. Program evaluations can be based on both quantitative information, such as records and statistics, and qualitative information, such as what people say about the programs. How your planning team decides to proceed should be based on the suitability, time, and cost of each option.

Some of the more traditional approaches include evaluating financial documents and ratios and other quantitative data. You can also conduct personal interviews, focus groups, or survey research to solicit ideas and opinions from the trustees, staff members, and other people throughout the school community. You then can compare and contrast those different viewpoints and identify areas of consensus.

Because your resources for this purpose will probably be limited, the key challenge is to determine how much information really is needed and from whom you should get it. For example, when developing surveys, you might want to develop streamlined survey formats that can be widely distributed to many different audiences, yet still be manageable enough for processing. One way to capture data relevant to your institution is to use the NAIS Parent Satisfaction Survey, Alumni Survey, and Climate Survey, which NAIS will offer through the Independent School Survey Builder, to be launched in Spring 2007. Watch *www.nais.org* for details.

While you want to gather the perspectives of many of the people closest to the school and most knowledgeable about its operations, you also want to avoid getting stuck in old assumptions. You want to make sure you get truly fresh views and perspectives that can be useful in rethinking how you want to move forward. Traditional assessment tools, such as focus groups and surveys, have an inherent problem, because they are limited by the knowledge of their participants, which can often be steeped in conventional wisdom. The key to grasping the future is to *get beyond* conventional wisdom.

Similarly, most school leaders are familiar with "SWOT" analysis for identifying critical issues and how well the organization is positioned to deal with them. Through SWOT, your school would gather information about its internal strengths ("S") and weaknesses ("W"), as well as the potential opportunities ("O") and threats ("T") that may influence it in the future. The trouble with SWOT is that it does not go far enough. After identifying SWOT, organizations need to attack aggressively all of their organizational and market assumptions. Thus, we recommend some additional ways to assess your position.

ANALYZING YOUR SCHOOL'S PORTFOLIO OF SERVICES

One newer method is portfolio analysis. It was created by Dr. Ian C. McMillan of the Wharton School of the University of Pennsylvania. It is intended to provide a way to determine which products and services of an organization should be amplified or eliminated, and how quickly. All independent schools, even the smallest, are involved in more than one service or activity. Thus, all independent schools have a "portfolio" of programs. During a time of cutbacks and scarce resources, the process of portfolio analysis can help you determine which aspects of your school's operations are most viable and essential. The analysis consists of a questionnaire that is deceptively simple, but that requires a thorough understanding of your own and your competitors' financial position.

Indicators of School Quality

Instructional and organizational effectiveness can be charted in the following categories:

- Curriculum;

- Instructional Strategies and Learning Activities;

- Assessment of Student Learning;

- Educational Agenda of the School: Vision, Beliefs, Mission and Goals;

- Leadership (for example, data-driven and research-based decision-making);

- Community-building (for example, fostering community-building conditions and working relationships within the school and the broader community);

- Culture of Continuous Improvement and Learning (for example, creating the conditions that support productive change and improvement).

For each of these categories, the National Study of School Evaluation provides research-based principles and types of evidence indicating that those principles are at work in a school.

— School Improvement: Focusing on Student Performance *(National Study of School Evaluation, Illinois, 1997)*

In portfolio analysis, your planning committee should: (1) group your school's activities and services according to its core businesses, support functions, and money makers; (2) compare them with your mission statement; (3) define your various products and services; and (4) ask the following questions of each program or service:

- Is it a good fit with other programs?

- Is it easy or difficult to implement?

- Is there high or low alternative coverage (meaning, do many other schools offer it or not)?

- Is our competitive position strong or weak?

The criteria for a good fit include congruence with the mission and purpose of the school, as well as the ability to draw on existing skills and share resources with other school activities. Ideally, your school will have two types of programs: well-fitting, easy programs, where you have a strong competitive position; and well-fitting, difficult programs that few other schools offer and that you have the strong capability to provide.

You should be evaluating programs that serve your school's mission and those that provide revenue. The programs that have the primary purpose of providing financial support should be evaluated according to the same rigorous market analysis that the programs of any private-sector business might use. You also should apply portfolio analysis to mission-driven activities to make sure that they are self-supporting, if possible, and operated efficiently, if not.

Independent schools tend to shy from viewing their academic programs as products and services, yet they are. For example, in an NAIS pilot project on a program-measurement system, one participating school considered eliminating German from its foreign language curriculum in favor of Japanese, because Japanese was viewed as a more useful and attractive offering to its customers, who are the students and their parents.

Helpful Information for Evaluating Your School

in Brief

- A copy of the current statement of mission and philosophy

- A copy of the last strategic or long-range plan

- A summary of the report of the last accreditation visit, if recent

- Budget results (in major categories)

- The tuition scale

- Salary ranges

- The number of faculty members

- Faculty-student ratio

- Information on financial aid and change over time

- The size of the student body, the applicant pool, and number of students accepted and enrolled

- Figures on student attrition

- Significant changes in curriculum

- A list of the next-level schools that graduates attend

- Community demographics and economic indicators

- Comparative data from peer independent schools and local private schools

— *Susan C. Stone*, Shaping Strategy *(NAIS, 1993)*

WAR GAMING IN A COMPETITIVE ENVIRONMENT

Another way to determine the viability of your school's offerings in a fiercely competitive environment is war gaming. Joseph Schumpeter, the early-20th-century economist who was famous for his lifecycle S-curve theory, said that everything — products, technologies, organizations, markets, nations — grows, matures, and dies under the constant challenge of the new. He called this "creative destruction," and he believed it could be harnessed to assure future institutional relevance. However, it takes courage not only to confront but also to plot your institution's demise and the products and systems you hold dear.

In the war-game approach, you convene a small group of customers and staff leaders to identify your school's most serious competitors. Members of the group then behave like the school's competitors would in order to systematically create the best strategies and tactics for destroying the institution's value and income streams.

The "attackers" should not be fettered by cost and practicality. Many competitors have vast resources. They will do whatever is necessary, once they target a market or product niche, to capture territory. The object of the attack group is to find chinks in the strongest parts of your school, to make obsolete the most cherished offerings, and to treat the institution's greatest assets as its greatest liabilities.

Once the most vulnerable areas have been identified, the attack group members should reverse their roles in order to erect defenses or end-run strategies to counter the competitive onslaught. Like the mythical Phoenix bird that destroyed itself and rose renewed from its own ashes, this process of creative destruction can resurrect and renew an organization.

IDENTIFYING YOUR CUSTOMERS' CUSTOMERS

Another method for analyzing competition is Customers' Customer Analysis©. It is designed to help organizations break out of limiting smokestack thinking, and evolve a more holistic vision that includes commercial factors and public policies influencing their environments beyond immediate parochial concerns.

The traditional analyses that guide most strategic planning tend to be predominantly introspective and only consider how you and your competitors within your own sector — in this case, the K-12 school sector — will be impacted by new technologies, customers, or competitors. This wider scope recognizes the simple fact that most changes, challenges, and opportunities that define market sectors usually come from outside existing market boundaries. To effectively evaluate an institution's potential, a Customers' Customer Analysis© looks at activities in competing and even alternative sectors.

For example, the technologies that currently are reshaping the convention industry came from experiments in distance learning in colleges and universities and from corporate teleconferencing. Changes in healthcare practices are being driven more by lifestyle changes in the home and the workplace than by technological breakthroughs in the labs. In education, there is increasing discussion about the use of video-game technologies as teaching tools. Could this bring Sony®, Nintendo®, and the division of Microsoft® Xbox into independent school education?

THE BALANCED SCORECARD

Environmental and internal assessments can be used to identify and prioritize the key issues confronting your school. That process will be discussed in Chapter 6. You also can use them as litmus tests of the validity of your school's mission, and as guides to help you determine other aspects of your strategic plan— for example, the types of indicators, metrics, and measurements that you should put into place to determine if your strategic plan is on track.

One of the newer ways to do this is through the "balanced scorecard" system of program measurement, which highlights four areas that can give trustees and administrators a more "balanced" perspective of their school's situation and progress. The four areas are financial measures, customer-satisfaction measures, process measures, and skills and knowledge measures. The concept was presented in the early 1990s in an article published in the *Harvard Business Review* and written by Robert S. Kaplan and David P. Norton. The concept now is being applied in both for-profit and nonprofit organizations.

Over time, these metrics have developed into a more dynamic relationship, because change in one metric influences the others. To reach a financial objective, your school may have to offer your students something new of value, which must be produced by an efficient process that is dependent on innovative people and skills.

The metrics can be applied to each program at your school, so that you can develop roadmaps that integrate important elements of your external and internal assessment. For example, if video gaming became a major teaching tool, it could potentially affect the four quadrants of the balanced scorecard in some of the following ways:

THE STRATEGIC PROCESS

- Financial measures: Cost of implementation, cost of marketing, revenue generated by the new technology;

- Customer (student/parent) satisfaction measures: Perception of value, quality of delivery, effectiveness of the tool;

- Process measures: Involvement of suppliers, status of delivery systems, integration into the curriculum;.

- Skills and knowledge measures: Acceptance by faculty and administration, training of faculty, and measurements of staff learning and innovation.

One approach is to gather information and data that allow you to evaluate your school's current situation as well as to measure its progress in the future based on those four metrics. For example, one organization has organized 12 strategic priorities into three major themes, which include organizational effectiveness, knowledge management, and advancing the profession.

Similarly, your school could identify its 10 to 15 major undertakings, based on major budget allocations. These might include programs, faculty, administration, physical plant, marketing, technology, and other areas. By gathering specific data and surveying various constituencies about your financial performance, your customers, your processes, and skills in each area, you can assess your progress. From that assessment, your planning committee can identify four or five priority projects each year.

IN CONCLUSION

Just as it's important to scan the internal environment, your school must also look inside to evaluate its performance in terms of serving its key constituencies and managing its operations. Traditional assessment tools — focus groups, surveys, personal interviews — can provide some good information, but newer methods can help your school think outside the box. Some of those methods include portfolio analysis, war gaming, Customer's Customer Analysis©, and the balanced scorecard approach.

After your school has done its internal evaluation and external assessment, it should have gathered enough information so that the school's leaders and planning committee can begin work on the next phase of the planning process, which is agreeing on priorities and identifying the key issues.

SWOT Analysis

One of the most familiar qualitative information-gathering tools is SWOT analysis. SWOT focuses on strengths, weaknesses, opportunities, and threats. When conducting a SWOT analysis, note that the "S" and the "W" are internal factors and the "O" and "T" are external factors. When compiling SWOT information, you should hone your list of possibilities to the top three strengths, weaknesses, opportunities, and threats indicated by each constituency group. Then you can organize your data in a matrix by constituency group as a way to search for themes. Themes that occur across groups point to potential core competencies, debilitating weaknesses, and strategic drivers.

— *Christina Drouin, founder and executive director, Center for Strategic Planning,*
  www.planonline.org.

ADDITIONAL
MATERIALS

Questions on Internal Scanning

Through internal research and scanning, your school can obtain relevant information about your key constituencies' expectations and satisfaction levels, your institution's governance concerns, and your organizational effectiveness. Here is a sampling of key questions that you might ask in each area:

Internal constituencies: What added value do we bring to our students' learning experience? How do we bring value to all our internal relationships, partnerships, and collaborations? What are the expectations and satisfaction levels of board, faculty, staff, administration, students, current parents, alumni, and parents of alumni? What do these constituencies think our school stands for?

What do these constituencies think of our school's overall effectiveness? What will our constituents expect of us over the next three to five years? How well are we prepared to meet those expectations? Who else is able to meet them as well or better than we can? What are our core competencies? That is to say, what one or two things do we excel at? Are these things that: a) we have excelled at for a long time, b) we can continue to excel at, c) our current and future markets value, and d) others would find hard to imitate?

Governance: Does the board operate strategically? How is the board organized? What do board members see as the critical issues? How does the board work with strategic topics such as succession planning, selection, performance evaluation, and sustainability?

Organizational: What structures and processes are working best to produce desired outcomes in behaviors, school climate, and culture? Which could use improvement? What are our values, and are they aligned with our institutional and individual actions? Do we have a marketing plan that goes beyond enrollment marketing to institutional marketing? How do we define and measure the success of our graduates? How do we plan for change? Continuous improvement? How do we evaluate ourselves? How do we prioritize and make decisions? Do we have a five-year financial strategic plan?

— *Christina Drouin, founder and executive director, Center for Strategic Planning, www.planonline.org.*

The EEMO²™ Survey for Self-Assessment

A tool that can be used to identify how effectively the organization is managed and what specific areas need attention is "Elements of an Effectively Managed Organization" (EEMO²™). EEMO²™ is a framework for looking at what it means to be effectively managed, and it can be used by an organization's managers to identify areas that are perceived as strengths and areas that are real or potential perceived weaknesses. EEMO²™ looks in depth at four dimensions of an organization:

1. **Mission.** How well are we achieving our mission, and how could we have greater impact?

2. **Finances.** Are our operations financially viable, and how can we ensure the long-term financial stability of our organization? Do we have effective financial-management systems in place to monitor our finances?

3. **Administrative capacity.** Do we have the administrative capacity to effectively and efficiently support our programs and services? What would it take to maximize our organizational capabilities in terms of planning, human resources, and leadership, organization culture and communication, and our technology and facilities infrastructure?

4. **Governance.** How effective is the board at protecting the public's interest, ensuring that charitable dollars are used effectively and efficiently and that the organization is fulfilling its mission? What can we do to ensure that our board is able to fulfill its governance role now and for the future?

— *Michael Allison and Jude Kaye,* Strategic Planning for Nonprofit Organizations *(second edition, John Wiley & Sons, 2005). The book also includes a sample of the EEMO²™ assessment tool.*

Deciding Where You Want To Go

You've gathered lots of insightful information: Now, how do you use it to plan for the future? What process should you use to determine your school's priorities, vision, and means of achieving that vision? In the following section, Christina Drouin, founder and executive director of the Center for Strategic Planning in Boca Raton, FL, provides information on:

■ How to identify the key strategic issues confronting your school;

■ Why you should revisit your core values and mission;

■ How to create a vision of success for the future;

■ What process you should use to identify your school's key goals, strategies, and initiatives; and

■ What measures to put in place to track the success of your planning efforts.

Section **III**

5 REVIEWING YOUR VALUES AND MISSION

By Christina Drouin, Founder and Executive Director, Center for Strategic Planning

The focus of your strategic plan should be the vision of what success looks like for your school in the future based on resolving the most crucial issues that it faces. To arrive at that vision, you must deal with those issues in a way that is consistent with your school's existing identity. Thus, you must first determine your core values and mission. How can you know what success looks like (vision), if you don't know why you exist (mission)? How do you know why you exist, if you don't know what you stand for (core values)?

Your strategic plan should embody and put into practice the handful of quintessential beliefs that define the school and what it stands for — the bedrock ideals to which the school community ascribes value above and beyond all else. As James C. Collins and Jerry I. Porras observed in *Built To Last: Successful Habits of Visionary Companies* (HarperCollins, 1994), such "core values are the organization's essential and enduring tenets — a small set of timeless guiding principles that require no external justification; they have intrinsic value and importance to those inside the organization." Values are "core" if they are so fundamental and deeply held that they will change seldom, if ever.

Core values encourage harmony within your school. Strategic plans that are anchored in core values will produce programs, projects, activities, and actions that are aligned with the ideals and purpose of the school. Together with mission, your core values establish your identity.

At NAIS, for example, the articulated core purpose and values are the four "I's" of independence, interdependence, inclusivity, and innovation. For a school, core values might be any of those and others such as love of learning, diversity, respect, trust, moral courage, honor, leadership, personal achievement, citizenship, excellence, child-centeredness, or service.

ARTICULATING CORE VALUES

Core values are indispensable to strategic planning, because they allow you to move forward while holding on to what you care about most. On a daily operational basis, core values help translate your school's ideals into specific behaviors and actions about how people are treated, how your school is led and managed, how decisions are made, and the quality of your school's programs and services. Applying core values will help you align actions with beliefs, establish priorities, sustain your school's integrity in times of change, and create your desired campus climate and culture. The articulation of core values can inspire commitment, establish expectations, and build a solid foundation for strong relationships with external constituencies — prospective families, donors, strategic partners in the community, and others.

Independent schools with articulated and claimed core values:

■ Know who they are and what defines them;

■ Are clear about what matters;

■ Use core values to inform their mission as well as strategic and daily decision-making about behaviors, relationships, services, and performance;

■ Seek to attract, retain, and form partnerships with individuals and groups that share those values; and

■ Can make operational decisions by department, division, or group while remaining strategically aligned with the overall mission of the school.

If your school has not formally identified its core values, you should take some specific steps to do that. First, you should select someone from the strategic planning team to organize and facilitate groups within and outside the school to identify what they believe are your school's core values. Whether that is part of the formal planning retreat, workshop, or in separate meetings, it must be done. Conducting such conversations is a key step in building a future that resonates throughout your school community. The goal of probing core values with different constituency groups is to build a foundation for future decision-making and planning. In addition, it gives those who participate the opportunity to understand fundamental truths about your school and their role in upholding them.

While comments from all constituencies can be useful, you should gather information from at least five key groups: your trustees, faculty, staff, administrative leadership, and alumni or founders. Gathering the views of those groups will help the strategic planning team determine which of the many values that are

Sample Core Values

Fort Worth Country Day School, Fort Worth, TX: Integrity, kindness, courage, respect, responsibility, scholarship.

Horace Mann School, Riverdale, NY: The life of the mind, mature behavior, mutual respect, a secure and healthful environment, a balance between individual achievement and a caring community.

important to your institution are its defining values: the fundamental ideals and standards that, if absent, would change the essence and character of your school.

This discovery process identifies what those values are, not what people want them to be. As James C. Collins warns in his article, "Aligning Actions and Values" in *Leader to Leader* magazine (Summer 1996), "You cannot 'set' organizational values, you can only discover them. Nor can you 'install' new core values into people. Core values are not something people 'buy into.' People must be predisposed to holding them.... The task is to find people who are already predisposed to sharing your core values. You must attract and then retain these people and let those who aren't predisposed to sharing your core values go elsewhere."

You should use a consistent technique across all constituency groups when conducting conversations about core values. One simple exercise involves convening small groups by constituency and posing the question, "What three things does this school stand for, or ascribe worth to, above all else?" You should record and discuss responses from each member of the group, identify recurrent themes, and narrow the list to three to five values on which the groups can agree.

Another exercise in discovering core values is the "Mars Group" that Collins describes in the same *Leader to Leader* article. It goes like this: "Imagine you've been asked to recreate the very best attributes of your organization on another planet, but you only have seats on the rocketship for five to seven people. Who would you send? They are probably the people who have a gut-level understanding of your core values, have the highest credibility with their peers, and demonstrate the highest levels of competence. Invariably they [do] a super job of articulating the core values precisely because they are exemplars of those values."

EVALUATING POSSIBLE CORE VALUES

As you gain information from different groups, you should develop a matrix of all the results that tell the planning team what key constituents identify as the school's key values, and where the institution's behavior reinforces or deviates from those values.

During any exercise that probes for core values, you must also make sure that what participants name as a core value is not simply a way that the school practices its values by its behaviors or ways of doing things. Collins gives an example of that in his "Aligning Actions and Values" article: "If I suggest that academic institutions should seriously think about changing the tenure system, the average academic is likely to say, 'Never! You're violating our core values.' But that protest arises from a failure to distinguish between values and practices. The core value is freedom of inquiry; tenure is a practice."

Collins warns that institutions can cling to what they think are basic values that are actually just habits — thus, failing to alter behaviors that they should change. "Your core values and purpose, if properly conceived, remain fixed," Collins explains. "Everything else — your practices, strategies, structures, systems, policies, and procedures — should remain open to change."

Once you have gathered data from the conversations among constituency groups, your strategic planning team should meet to review, discuss, and analyze the findings, and then agree on three to five core values that resonate most throughout all the groups. To determine those values, the team should ask itself the following questions:

- Does this value reflect a defining aspect of the true nature of our school? Is this what really matters at our school?
- Can this value act as a foundation for our school's mission and vision?
- Is this value timeless — can it transcend changes in administration, leadership, and market conditions? Can you see living with it for 100 years?

You are seeking to identify the few values that have brought your institution to where it is today and will, in the words of Collins and Porras, "preserve the core" even as you seek to "stimulate progress" and secure the future.

WRITING CORE VALUES STATEMENTS

After your school has agreed upon its core values, the planning team should appoint a work group to develop statements that express the way that your school should live those values through its educational, operational, and social structures. For example, if one of your core values is diversity, then your core values statement might express that your school "seeks, nurtures, and embraces diversity. Distinguished by our long-standing tradition of celebrating one another's differences, we continue to strive toward a better understanding of the world." If one of your core values is honor, then your values statement might say, "The concept of personal honor is an enduring and immutable standard by which we tell others how we want to be measured. Once developed, personal honor is the benchmark by which to judge all our actions." And if one of your core values is community, then your statement might be, "We value relationships that connect us to each other and to the larger world. We aspire to be a nurturing community that respects the dignity of every human being."

You should also apply the following tests to your core values statements:

- Do these statements capture the essence of our school?
- Do these statements describe us at our best?
- Will these statements guide decision-making in the daily and long-term delivery of our school's mission?
- Will these statements create and sustain alignment, especially in times of change?
- Can these statements live with us indefinitely?

If the answer is yes to all five, then you are well on your way to establishing the first building block of your formal strategic plan.

COMMON QUESTIONS ABOUT CORE VALUES

What if our school has already identified its core values?

Use them! Incorporate them as cornerstones in your planning process. Distribute them to all your constituencies, and display them in prominent places throughout the school. Incorporate them into hiring packets, new-employee orientation sessions, and admissions materials. Review them at the first faculty meeting of the year. Hold regular discussions about the challenges posed by trying to live those values over the past semester or year, and share ideas for overcoming any obstacles to putting them into practice. Test for alignment.

For each core value, ask the question, "If this is what we say we stand for, what is the evidence that our actions match this belief?" Rate responses on a numeric scale to measure congruency. To improve your scores, brainstorm lists of things that your school can do that give further evidence of each belief in action. Then, send your brainstormed lists to the strategic planning team.

What if we can't agree on our core values?

If that's the case, your school has an identity issue that you must resolve. With no common ground, building consensus and community are nearly impossible. Independent schools that are in this situation usually have trouble resolving conflicts, identifying priorities, and forming relationships inside and outside the institution. You need to go back to your foundation and identify the one or two beliefs on which there is agreement. Once you discover the shared common ground, you can start to build on that.

What if an important value is missing?

Values can't simply be grafted onto an organization as an afterthought. Still, it is not impossible for astute leadership to identify an important emerging value that most people within the school community agree should be part of the school's belief system or culture, but is not yet identified. You can aspire to hold that value and begin to establish structures and processes that will encourage behaviors and decisions consistent with that value. Over time, the school's culture will begin to reflect it.

DEVELOPING A MISSION STATEMENT BASED ON VALUES

Most independent schools have a mission statement, and you have probably already invested significant time and effort in crafting one. As part of your strategic planning process, you should consider the mission statement in new ways and review it for clarity, brevity, and focus. Your school would be well served by devising a simplified, one- or two-sentence statement of your mission that is easy for people throughout the school community to understand and remember. Also, as Bruce Butterfield, president of The Forbes Group, has observed, "The main value of a mission is as a filter of activities. Consequently, it should be more exclusive than inclusive. A mission that is too broad is a wide-open door to lack of focus."

You also should ensure that the mission statement is congruent with the core values that you've identified. That will require you to shift your discussion of a mission statement from *what* you do to *why* you do what you do. In other words, you should redefine your mission along the lines of purpose — the end result that your school wants to accomplish — rather than specific activities. For example, you might ask yourselves two key questions, as suggested by Jim Collins and Jerry I. Porras in an article in the *Harvard Business Review,* "Building your Company's Vision" (September/October 1996): "What would be lost if this organization ceased to exist?" And "Why is it important for this organization to exist?"

In their book, *The Facilitator's Fieldbook* (American Management Association, 1999), Tom Justice and David W. Jamieson propose several other questions that you might answer to help define your mission and purpose. After determining why you exist, you should consider who your primary beneficiaries are. Whom do you exist to serve? Resulting in what outcomes? Based on what beliefs?

An exemplary school mission statement should flow from core values and be clear, understandable, enduring, and focused. It should be internalized by the campus community, to the extent that it guides long-term and daily decisions in every aspect of school life. It should inspire the loyalty and passion of anyone associated with your institution. In short, you should reconsider your mission along the following dimensions:

- Does the mission statement answer the question "Why do we exist?"
- Is it consistent with core values?
- Is it clear, understandable, and memorable?
- Will it endure?
- Will it serve as a basis for operational as well as strategic decision-making?
- Does it give all who see it or hear it a compelling reason to support your school?

Then, considering the answers to all those questions, you should decide if and how your mission statement should be changed.

In addition, although most independent schools have mission statements, few divisions, committees, academic and administrative departments, or other planning units or groups do. Articulating individual missions can be useful to help each planning unit carry out your institutional strategic plan, once it has been developed. If a division, department, or group can answer the question of why it exists in ways that support the overall mission of the school, then it is in a far better position to contribute to the school's vision and goals as expressed in its strategic plan.

WRITING YOUR VALUES-BASED MISSION STATEMENT

You should designate one or two writers from the planning committee to review and revise your current mission statement in light of the core values that you have identified and the tests of the mission that I've described. If the mission statement needs revision, the writers can present their version of a new mission statement to the planning committee, which can then send it to your trustees for ratification.

A Hierarchy of Statements

Independent school mission statements vary widely, partly because of the varied nature of the schools, and partly because of a general blurring of the disparate concepts of mission, philosophy, purpose, goals, and objectives, and the fact that these concepts seem to have little uniform meaning from one school to the next.

Schools are now developing a hierarchy of statements, including the following components:

A mission statement or statement of purpose that addresses succinctly the questions of why the school exists and whom it should serve. (The responsibility of the board.)

A philosophy statement or statement of creed that addresses the overarching principles upon which the school operates, including, but not restricted to, methodology/pedagogy, school structure, climate, and curricular emphasis. Often the philosophy or creed statement affirms the underlying principles of the school and its pedagogy: "This we believe…" (Developed by the board, administration, and faculty.)

A goals statement that addresses the principal outcomes you should expect from the experience of the school. (Developed by the board, administration, and faculty.)

Objectives, developed by division, department, grade-level, teacher, and course. (Developed by the faculty at the divisional and departmental levels, and often appearing in a separate curriculum guide.)

When such a hierarchy of statements exists, there is a greater likelihood of involvement in defining the goals and accountability across several levels of the school community. NAIS believes that asking the various groups indicated to take separate responsibility tends to produce more sharply focused and integrated statements than the single, all-encompassing, committee-written statement of philosophy that too often ends up looking like the proverbial camel (the "horse designed by committee").

— *Patrick F. Bassett, NAIS President*

IN CONCLUSION

Your strategic plan should embody and put into practice the handful of quintessential ideals, beliefs, and standards that define the school, what it stands for, and to which the school community ascribes worth above and beyond everything else. Core values inform both strategic and daily decision-making in ways that build community and help create a healthy organization where actions mirror beliefs. Articulating and practicing core values will help establish priorities, sustain your school's integrity in times of change, and create your desired campus climate and culture.

You also should ensure that the mission statement is congruent with the core values that you've identified. It may require several drafts to develop the final statement, but it will be well worth the time and effort. Consider the words of Frances Hesselbein, chairman of the board of governors of the Drucker Foundation, in the article, "Carry a Big Basket" in *Leader to Leader* magazine (Spring 2002): "If we are to be relevant in an uncertain age, then abandoning those things that do not further the mission is a leadership imperative....If it doesn't further the mission, over the side it goes. Mission focus gets us where we want to go. For many leaders, the destination is where work, people, and challenge converge — mobilizing around mission, changing lives, building community, and coming home. In these turbulent, often violent times, we recall with certitude that 'it is the set of the sails and not the gales that determine the way we go.'"

ADDITIONAL
MATERIALS

Sample Values Statements

Miss Hall's School, Pittsfield, MA

Authenticity

At MHS, we are committed to helping each girl to develop, test, comprehend, and act from her own spirit, core values, abilities, expertise, and judgment.

Honor

The concept of personal honor is an enduring and immutable standard by which we tell others how we want to be measured. Once developed, personal honor is the benchmark by which to judge all our actions.

Respect

Respect for others begins with respect for self. Respect for others extends beyond tolerance to include active concern for and service to others.

Growth

We value challenge in a nurturing environment. We also value curiosity, clear thinking, and academic accomplishment. We encourage the development of resilience, determination, and self-confidence for a lifetime of learning in a world of constant change.

Saint Mary's School, Raleigh, NC

Excellence in Teaching and Learning

We value the transformational growth that takes place when teachers and students experience the joy of learning together. A collaborative academic culture nurtures intellectual courage, curiosity, and creativity.

Personal Achievement in Mind, Body, and Spirit

We value intellectual, physical, and spiritual wholeness. We inspire young women to discover their talents, pursue their passions, and achieve their personal best.

Honor

We value honor and integrity as central to building character. Our individual and shared commitment to honor, embodied in the Honor Code, creates a foundation of trust and respect essential to an ethical and moral life.

Community

We value relationships that connect members of the school community to each other and to the larger world. We aspire to be a nurturing community that respects the dignity of every human being.

Heritage

We cherish and celebrate our heritage, one that is rich in tradition, Episcopal values, and opportunity for women. The best of our past forms the foundation for the best of our future.

Sample Mission Statements

Cheshire Academy, Cheshire, CT

Believing in the value of each human being and the richness of a diverse community, Cheshire Academy exists to provide a quality educational experience in a caring environment where individuals take responsibility for their personal growth so that they can reach their full potential and make a difference in the world.

Saint Andrew's School, Boca Raton, FL

Saint Andrew's School is an Episcopal K-12 day and boarding college preparatory school whose mission is to build a community of learners, to provide excellence in education, and to nurture the whole child in mind, body, and spirit.

McLean School of Maryland, Potomac, MD

McLean makes education accessible, stimulating, and meaningful for a broad range of learners.

Our students flourish because McLean responds to students' learning styles.

McLean prepares students intellectually and socially by encouraging self-advocacy and building self-confidence.

Our students succeed because they learn how to learn.

Baylor School, Chattanooga, TN

Baylor's mission is to foster in its students both the ability and the desire to make a positive difference in the world.

Phillips Exeter Academy, Exeter, NH

Exeter seeks to graduate people whose creativity and independence of thought sustain continuing inquiry and reflection, whose interest in others and in the world around them surpasses their self-concern, and whose passion for learning impels them beyond what they already know.

Saint Margaret's Episcopal School, San Juan Capistrano, CA

Our mission at St. Margaret's Episcopal School is to educate the hearts and minds of young people for lives of learning, leadership, and service.

The Kinkaid School, Houston, TX

Kinkaid's mission is to promote educational excellence, personal responsibility, and balanced growth, and thereby to help its students to discover and develop their talents and to fulfill their best potentials.

Lakeside School, Seattle, WA

The mission of Lakeside School is to develop in intellectually capable young people the creative minds, healthy bodies, and ethical spirits needed to contribute wisdom, compassion, and leadership to a global society.

We provide a rigorous, academic program through which effective educators lead students to take repsonsibility for learning.

We are committed to sustaining a school in which individuals representing diverse cultures and experiences instruct one another in the meaning and value of community and in the joy and importance of lifelong learning.

IS IMPORTANT
TO prioritize

6 IDENTIFYING THE KEY ISSUES THAT CONFRONT YOUR SCHOOL

By Christina Drouin, Founder and Executive Director, Center for Strategic Planning

Your school's strategic plan ultimately should help resolve any major challenges that are likely to influence the school's performance and viability over the next several years. Thus, an important step in your planning process is to identify those issues that you think will have the most impact — positive or negative — in shaping your school's future. Such issues, whether they are referred to as strategic drivers, critical issues, or strategic issues, should be those that are directly connected to your school's core values, mission, and core competencies — those that are crucial to the future sustainability of the school.

The process that you use can vary, depending on how you want to approach the assignment. You might want the planning committee to do the main part of the work and then present the three to five key issues that they've identified in the form of a white paper at a one-day or weekend workshop, where representatives of all your main constituency groups can review those issues. As an alternative, you may present the findings from your internal and external research directly to your key constituencies at the workshop, and then make identifying the key issues the first order of business for those who are gathered there. Either way, the information must be shared and discussed broadly.

How often you identify the issues that are influencing your school can vary as well. Some independent schools identify their key issues every several years, but current thinking encourages you to review them on an annual basis to make sure your priorities reflect today's realities.

THE STRATEGY-MAKING WORKSHOP

As Marc Frankel and Judith Schechtman highlighted in the first chapter of this book, you might organize a meeting at some site away from the school, where those who are most invested in your institution can spend time reassessing where it has been and where it needs to go.

One approach would be to hold an extensive brainstorming workshop among 25 to 30 people from the board, the planning committee, and any other key players from other constituencies for one or two days. Prior to that session, the planning committee would circulate to the attendees the results of any preliminary data. Then, the workshop, led by a planning consultant or facilitator, if possible, would focus on the following:

- Analysis of survey results and consultant reports;
- Assessment of the identified internal and external factors that can impact your school;
- Presentation of planning team's white paper on what it sees as the key issues to consider;
- Review of core values and mission;
- Development of a shared vision of the future;
- The setting of goals and crafting of strategies.

Another approach would be to accomplish the first four steps in smaller groups — for example, within the planning committee of the board or at meetings with various other stakeholder groups. Then, having obtained that information, you would focus on the final two steps in a visioning day (as described in Chapter 7). While it's important to have a workshop or retreat that gathers together people who care about the school to help plan its strategy, you can and should determine when and how that will occur based on your school's specific situation.

DETERMINING THE ISSUES

Whatever approach you use, the first step in identifying the most crucial issues confronting your school is to connect the internal assessment of your school's situation with the results of your scan of the external environment. You should review both sets of strategic information in tandem, not isolation, because the two usually influence each other. For instance, even as a school's external environment affects its operations, the school can change that same environment by realizing its vision for the future.

You should consider the following three groups of questions when you analyze all the information that you've compiled from your internal evaluation and external assessment:

- What does our information point to as our core competencies and our market position? How will those be influenced by the changing needs and expectations of our constituents over the next three years?
- What environmental changes, issues, and trends might have the greatest impact on our ability to deliver on our core competencies and fulfill our mission over one to three years?
- How well are we aligned as an institution? In other words, are our strategic and daily decisions congruent with our core values and mission?

Your aim in gathering and analyzing all the information is to step back and identify the three to five specific issues that will have the greatest influence on your school in the future. Your planning team should begin with a search for recurring themes based on a review and analysis of your research findings. They should identify the top issues that emerge from focus groups, one-on-one interviews, external scanning, and other assessment and evaluation tools. Then, they can develop a matrix by naming the most commonly cited issues, or those internal or external forces that each constituency group thinks will have the biggest impact.

In *Strategic Planning for Nonprofit Organizations* (John Wiley & Sons, 1997), Michael Allison and Jude Kaye gave an example of the benefits of that effort. They pointed to an independent school that had spent much money, time, and other resources to diversify its student body for many years. "Yet, during an extensive series of focus groups and interviews, the school came to find out that the perception of the general population, and especially parents of potential enrollees, was that the school catered to white, upper-class families," they wrote. "The issue, 'how can we change the image of our school to more accurately reflect who we are,' was not initially listed as a strategic issue…but was added to the list of key questions that needed to be answered by the end of the strategic planning process."

As John M. Bryson notes in *Strategic Planning for Public and Nonprofit Organizations* (Jossey-Bass, 1995), there is a real art to framing issues. It is important to make sure that you are truly asking the fundamental policy questions and challenges that your school faces. Thus, he recommends that before your planning team settles on a final set of issues to address, it should ask the following questions:

- What is the issue?
- Why is it an issue?

- What, in terms of the mission or external and internal situation, makes it one?
- Can we do anything about it? What would happen if we didn't do anything about it?
- Can we combine or eliminate certain issues?
- Should we break issues down into several issues?
- Are there any issues missing from our list, especially those that our culture might make us overlook?
- Will strategies for resolving an issue require significant investments of time, money, and other resources?
- Who in the school community must deal with this issue?

Ultimately, you will want to shape the issues that you have identified into critical-issues statements or questions. For example, some strategic issues and their related questions might be:

Strategic Issue: 21st Century Curriculum

What does it mean to be an educated person in the 21st century? In what significant ways does your school's educational experience need to change in order to better prepare students as world citizens or global leaders?

Strategic Issue: Faculty Recruitment and Retention

What are the current and emerging issues concerning faculty recruitment and retention? What must your school do to meet challenges and take advantage of opportunities in order to attract, retain, and compensate highly qualified faculty and staff in an increasingly competitive market for talent and resources?

Strategic Issue: Marketing the School

If perceived image were to match desired image (brand identity), what would your school be known as? Where are the gaps? What must you do to bridge them? Is your positioning strategy working? What will be important to your brand and its market position in the future that has not been important in the past? How can you prepare?

PRIORITIZING ISSUES

Upon analyzing the results of internal and external research, you may find that your school faces more than a handful of strategic issues. From among them, it is important to prioritize those that you will deal with in this planning cycle. You can determine that priority in a number of ways, and your planning team must consider the implications of each on different aspects of your school.

Some Potential Strategic Issues in Independent Schools

Seeking financial sustainability. What financial model will effectively sustain the growth and development of a dynamic educational program over the next 10 years? What must you do to build such a model?

Achieving institutional alignment. What must change for your school to fully live up to its core values and mission? How can you create those changes?

Building community. What attributes and behaviors do you want your community to reflect? What must you start doing, stop doing, increase, or decrease to evolve into the community you desire?

Optimizing the role of alumni. How might the future be different, if alumni stayed connected with the school or were reconnected? What if you focused on alumni as a constituency? What would be the merits, impacts, and issues of a scenario where the school made significant progress in building alumni relations within the next one to three years?

Defining what students need to learn at the beginning of the 21st century. In what significant ways do you prepare students as educated individuals in the 21st century? What are the needs of your graduates, in terms of knowledge, skills, abilities, attitudes, behaviors, conditions, or status, while and after they attend your school?

In his book, Bryson describes an excellent approach to issues prioritization that he calls the direct approach. In the direct approach, planners go straight from the analysis of internal and external research to the identification of key issues. If you take that approach, the key questions that you should ask are:

- What is the issue?
- What external and internal factors make it an issue?
- What are the consequences of failing to deal with this issue?

Bryson also recommends determining which issues are most important over the short or long term, and to phrase each one as a challenge that your school can meet.

Using another approach, the planning team would consider which issues are most urgent for your school from both a direct-impact and macro level. Direct-impact issues are those that have an immediate effect on the school. Macro issues have a broader influence on the school's capabilities and outcomes. Thus, whereas recruiting faculty who are aligned with the mission of the school is a direct-impact issue, a national teacher shortage is a macro issue. Similarly, while the changing applicant pool in your area is a direct-impact issue, public perception of independent school education is a macro issue.

You should also watch for two critical intersections: Where a strategic issue impacts a core competency, or one of the key areas in which your school excels, and where it impacts its ability to fulfill its mission. Any issue that affects either should be a top priority.

WRITING ASSUMPTIONS

While the planning team members identify strategic issues, they should document the assumptions that they are making as they think about the future of the school relative to the issues at hand. Assumptions may be based on external conditions — such as social, technological, environmental, economic, and political concerns — as well as the school's internal status. The latter involves constituency needs and wants, enrollment projections, independent education market trends, the financial health of the school, issues in global education, and so on. It is important that the team is explicit about such planning assumptions, so they can be included in the school's written strategic plan and used as a tracking device for ongoing strategic thinking.

For example, if securing your school's financial future is a strategic issue, one underlying assumption that you would list is that there is a financial model that would work for your school. If marketing of your school is a strategic issue, you might write an assumption that there will continue to be markets and school products and services to develop, and that the demographics of your market area will remain the same or change according to projections, and so on.

If the underlying assumptions of your plan are documented clearly, they can serve as checkpoints to periodically test whether the strategy is still on point or if your plan needs adjusting. As Chapter 10 on recalibrating the plan will discuss, you may want to hold mini-workshops each year for your board or other key constituencies to come together for a half day to review the plan and its assumptions. An alternative would be to hold strategic thinking sessions more regularly with your board and administrators to ensure the plan remains current and on track.

In the end, based on the ideas and concerns that you've gathered from your key constituencies, the environmental scans, and the evaluation of current services through the balanced scorecard and other approaches, you are aiming to determine the strategic imperatives on which your school should focus over the next one to five years — knowing that an annual update and evaluation of imperatives may change those priorities because of new developments.

IN CONCLUSION

Through your internal and external evaluations, you will probably identify a wide range of issues that can influence your school in some way. To deal effectively with issues, however, you will need to prioritize them and focus your school's resources on those that will have the greatest impact. You should explore various methods to help pinpoint such issues and involve a broad range of constituencies in the process. Through that effort, your school will be able to create what Jim Collins has called the "envisioned future" that will become the school's top priority over the next one to five years.

7 CREATING YOUR VISION FOR THE FUTURE

By Christina Drouin, Founder and Executive Director, Center for Strategic Planning

What is your dream for your school? What do you see when you look at the horizon three to five years out?

As the next step in the planning process, your planning committee and key people throughout the school should analyze the potential effects of current and projected external forces, and they should develop scenarios as to how those forces may affect your institution. Most important, your institution should begin to articulate a vision of success. A vision is a word picture of the best possible future, one that pulls your school forward and, in the words of Jim Collins, "stimulates progress." The purpose of creating a vision is to inspire and guide actions that will make your school's idealized future a reality.

In your vision of success, do you see a school that is significantly different? Perhaps you have established important new partnerships that have enhanced your ability to deliver learning opportunities. Perhaps you have established a global learning community that has an international impact. Whatever your vision, is it shared? How does it compare to what others envision?

The vision should be the leading edge of your strategic plan. According to Frank Martinelli in *Strategic Planning Manual* (The Center for Public Skills Training, 1999), a vision should answer the question, "If we could create the school of our dreams, one that prevails over its critical issues and has the impact we most desire, what would it look like?" Your vision should be clear and memorable, and paint a compelling visual image that motivates people to action. It should reflect such a desired future state that anyone who learns of it will want to be part of creating it.

Your vision is not the same as your core values or mission, but it should flow from them. In fact, core values and mission are two sides of the same coin, and together they form your core ideology, as Jim Collins and Jerry I. Porras explain

THE STRATEGIC PROCESS

in *Built to Last: Successful Habits of Visionary Companies* (HarperCollins, 1994). If core values and mission form the conscience of your institution, vision constitutes the desire of its heart.

HOW VISION DIFFERS FROM MISSION

While your mission statement tells your purpose, your vision statement should suggest your destination. Mission gives daily relevance to your works, and it preserves the school's purpose and what it stands for. Even as you consider the future resolution of strategic issues, you also must preserve the essence of the institution. In contrast, vision inspires stretching beyond the norm. It's your vision of progress that helps you improve and gives future sustainability to your mission. Values and mission remain constant, while visions change as they are achieved.

The vision should be challenging but also obtainable. It is easy to end up with a vision that is either too restricted or too encompassing. If it's too restricted, it won't be compelling enough to excite, motivate, or inspire action. If it's too encompassing, it will become meaningless in its generality.

Thus, when developing a vision statement, you should ask the following questions:

- Is it a vivid description of a desired future that is a dramatic stretch from where the school is today?
- Is it clear, understandable, and memorable?
- Does it inspire passion, compel action, and serve as a rallying call?
- Is it consistent with school values and mission?
- Does it set a clear direction and create alignment in decision-making across the institution?
- When realized, will it resolve the school's strategic issues?

VISIONING TOOLS FOR GROUP PROCESS

How can you best involve a wide variety of constituencies in developing a shared vision for your school? In addition to conducting sessions with key planning-team members in developing a vision statement, you should organize a much larger session or sessions that involve other key groups within and outside of the school. Visioning exercises should be a key activity in any major strategic planning process that your school organizes.

Several collaborative approaches can help the school community actively think about and articulate its future. They include:

Vision casting

Exercises in vision casting can include provocative group discussions, guided visualizations, and even literally drawing scenarios of the future. Some of the questions that you might ask your faculty members, administrators, students, and other key constituencies as you develop your vision include:

- How will we address the changing needs of our students as educated individuals in the 21st century?
- What impact do we want to have on our students, faculty, staff, administrators, and families? What do we want to be true of their awareness, skills, knowledge, behavior, attitude, or condition during and after their experience with us?
- Whom will we be serving three or five years from now — and how?
- What will our students, families, faculty, and staff members need from us over the next three to five years?
- What is the most important thing to accomplish over the next three to five years?
- What does success look like for us?
- How would our school need to progress to achieve these results?
- What will we be, and what will we be known for in five years, that we aren't known for today?

Representatives from your strategic planning team can work with your key constituencies to answer these questions and develop written visions based on their answers. They also can ask them to sketch or draw a vision for the future and share it with the rest of the participants. You will want to gather similarities that resonate with the group, eventually creating a composite of the group's shared vision.

The vision narrative

Vision statements are intended to paint a clear picture of a destination that your school will reach at an appointed time in the future. But can faculty and staff members, parents, students, and trustees articulate what the vision means to them personally? What role do they see themselves playing in that envisioned future? A vision narrative is a tool beyond the vision statement that adds richness and clarity, so that people can "see" themselves influencing that future vision.

To create a vision narrative, you should ask different people who represent each of your key groups to compose a short story about a person's encounter with the school, as each of them imagines it will be in five years. This could be from the point of view of a student, a parent, or a new faculty member. What will the school look like? Who will be doing what and why? How will things come together to produce the desired outcomes? The vision narrative is an in-depth story of the future told from various points of view. It can be several paragraphs or even several pages.

Scenario planning

School planners can also help build agreement on a vision by exploring hypothetical, alternative futures. If you take that approach, The Forbes Group has found a method, the Schwartz/GBN model, to be most effective. This model is named in recognition of Peter Schwartz, a co-founder and chairman of Global Business Network, an organization that specializes in scenario planning and futures research. The Schwartz/GBN model maximizes the scenarios' relevance to the issue or issues confronting an organization by limiting the change drivers to those with the greatest potential impact on the organization's most critical issues. The change drivers must influence each other and are displayed on two intersecting axes, which form a four-quadrant matrix where each quadrant is a future world to be described in a scenario.

The poles of the axes are opposite states and have a 50/50 chance of occurring. For example, in the days before Y2K, some people assumed that nothing much would happen when 1999 became 2000, while others bought desert property and loaded up on guns and food. The two change drivers were the severity of the technological impact and the human response to it. The vertical axis plotted the technology impact, and the horizontal axis plotted the human response. The poles of each axis were isolated failure versus widespread failure on the technology axis and social coherence versus social breakdown on the human-response axis.

The tough part is getting the change drivers narrowed down to two powerful ones that influence each other. The objective is not to select the best or most probable scenario, but to be able to respond flexibly and promptly and make better decisions. The scenario is not a prediction of the future, but a tool for thinking creatively about possible alternative future situations should they occur.

Appreciative Inquiry

You also might consider engaging your participants in Appreciative Inquiry (AI). As with all approaches to visioning, AI requires context. In this case, the context is provided by the school's stories of success as opposed to its problems. AI is an

Sample Stretch Vision Statements

Charlotte Latin School (Charlotte, NC)
Vision 2009 — Great Expectations

CLS will unite its legacy of academic excellence with a renewed commitment to the arts, athletics, leadership development, and character education to create a balanced learning environment that prepares our students to lead meaningful and fulfilling lives as it models educational leadership for other schools.

Donna Klein Jewish Academy (Boca Raton, FL)
Vision Statement for 2010

By 2010, in a state-of-the art facility, Donna Klein Jewish Academy will be a model of academic excellence where K–12 students celebrate learning, the richness of Jewish life, and Torah values.

International Community School (Decatur, GA)
Vision 2010

In the year 2010, ICS will be a multicultural village in which the school is the hub and the teacher is the heart — a community of learners and global citizens that thinks independently and works cooperatively.

McLean School of Maryland (Potomac, MD)
Vision 2003-2008 — Linking Today with Tomorrow

To be a model educational community committed to the individual learning styles of students.

organizational change management strategy originated by David Cooperrider and Suresh Srivastva in the 1980s. It is based on a paradigm that calls for a shift from traditional deficit-based change management to a positive approach. Organizations are not problems to be solved, but are centers of infinite human capacity — ultimately unpredictable, unknowable, or a "mystery alive," according to Cooperrider and Srivastva. "What is the best we have been?" becomes the key question rather than "What are our problems?"

At Case Western Reserve University's Appreciative Inquiry Commons website *(appreciativeinquiry.cwru.edu/intro/timeline.cfm),* Jane Magruder Watkins and Bernard Mohr chronicle an Appreciative Inquiry History and Timeline taken from their book *Appreciative Inquiry: Change at the Speed of Imagination* (Jossey-Bass/Pfeiffer, 2001). They write that Cooperrider and Srivastva "offer the hypothesis that human systems grow in the direction of what people study; therefore, let us all search for the true, the good, the better, and the possible in human systems." Over the years, AI has proven that positive things happen when an organization focuses on its successes and strengths rather than on its problems and weaknesses. Using this approach, a school that looks for and appreciates its successes, then applies them to addressing the challenges it is facing, can build a future where those successes are more common.

Cooperrider and Srivastva's 4-D approach to Appreciative Inquiry involves the following steps:

1. *Discover.* **Appreciate "The Best of What Is"**

    Task: Focus on experiences of excellence and use an interview process. Tell stories to one another of times when the organization is at its best.

2. *Dream.* **Envision "What Might Be"**

    Task: Focus on the data from interviews and create possible visions of the organization's future and potential impact as if the peak moments of excellence described in the "discover" phase have become the norm. Known as "provocative propositions," these visions can be developed by asking "what if?"

3. *Design.* **Consent to "What Should Be"**

    Task: Focus on the vision of the future and create the structure and process changes required to stimulate progress toward the vision.

4. *Destiny.* **Experience "What Can Be"**

    Task: Focus on the organizational design changes required by the envisioned future and implement what is needed to bring about the vision.

Based on the writing of Sue Annis Hammond in *The Thin Book of Appreciative Inquiry* (second edition, Thin Book Publishing, 1998), a series of Appreciative Inquiry probes for a school interested in building community might be:

> Think of an example of a time when you experienced this school as a genuine caring community. Tell a story of what happened. What made this experience effective? As you look to the future, describe one thing this school could do to heighten people's experience of this school as a genuine, caring community.

A school seeking to more fully live by its core values could pose the same series of probes for each value, resulting in a series of specific ideas for a vision.

In another example, schools using the Appreciative Inquiry approach to enhancing campus diversity could begin, not with the deficit discourse ("How are we failing in this arena?"), but with appreciating and valuing the best of what is ("What do we do well here?"), followed by dreaming of what might be ("What would it look like if the exceptions were the norm?"). Then, they would initiate the leveraging discussion ("How can we take what we do well to build structures and processes to achieve our diversity goals?"), and finally work together toward experiencing the promise of the possibilities.

CHALLENGES TO CREATING A VISION

Your school community may encounter certain common pitfalls when trying to create a shared vision. Some of the key challenges include:

Not considering the impact of environmental forces

Avoid the temptation to cut corners in the research area. It's crucial to scan and assess both your external environment and internal status so that you can understand what will probably be the biggest influences on your school's future. Your strategic planning team should set research parameters before beginning to create a vision for the school — and then stick to them.

Trying to budget before visioning

Nothing inhibits visionary thinking more than introducing budget concerns too soon in the process. Even though a common outcome of strategic planning is the information to support a campaign case statement, new sources of support are not the only enablers of vision. For example, changing structures, processes, attitudes, and behaviors — each as legitimate an aspect of vision as facilities, programs, or salaries — often have no hard costs attached to them. Vision and strategy should inform the budget, not vice versa.

Not getting enough buy-in

It is easy to think "Faculty members are already overloaded, and no one has time to participate in anything extra," or "People don't really care if they participate," or "It's more expedient for a small group of school leaders to create the plan, including the vision, and then to hand it off to other people to carry out." But that isn't the best approach.

You should always ask the key question: "What do we have to do in framing the strategic planning process to build trust and enthusiasm so other people will participate?" The effort that the planning team spends exploring that topic will be rewarded not only in building the plan but also in putting it into action. The best way to get participation on the back end, the implementation phase, is to get involvement on the front end.

IN CONCLUSION

The heart of any strategic planning process is to develop a vision of where you want your school to be in the future. The vision should not be the same as your values and mission, but it should flow from them — representing an idealized future in which your strategic issues have been resolved in a manner that is consistent with what your school stands for and why it exists. There are a number of exercises that can help your school and its key constituencies arrive at a strong and viable vision — one that will be a stretch and stimulate progress, pointing you toward the success you want in the years to come.

Yet visioning is not a wish-upon-a-star type of activity; it is a disciplined and collaborative exercise in strategic thinking and discernment. Management expert Peter Drucker put it this way in *Management: Tasks, Responsibilities, Practices* (Harper & Row, 1974): "Strategic planning does not deal with future decisions. It deals with the futurity of present decisions." By articulating your vision, you will be better able to set priorities. Only by knowing where you want to end up in the future will you be able to develop the roadmap for getting there.

ADDITIONAL
MATERIALS

Visioning Day at Independent Schools

Different schools will handle the strategic planning workshops that they conduct every few years differently. Some will use those workshops to check institutional alignment with values and mission, prioritize key strategic issues, and create a vision for the future, as well as to determine the supporting goals and strategies to reach that vision. Others will focus only on developing the vision and key goals to reach it. Some will want to include only their key leaders, while others will invite representatives of a wide range of groups. Whatever you chose, the hypothetical situation below describes the general steps involved in organizing a workshop.

In this particular case study, an independent school decides to focus its planning workshop on developing a shared vision and corresponding goals, and it wants to be as inclusive as possible in the process. It has taken that tack during its situational analysis phase through surveys, focus groups, interviews, and strategic-thinking sessions. Now, the planning team wants to carry that inclusivity into its visioning day and chooses an all-call approach that welcomes everyone to participate.

Who is in the room?

The planning team — aware that during the school's most recent planning process, a traditional representational approach was used — wants this process to extend the reach beyond a couple dozen people. Determined to cast a wider net, the planning team decides to make the planning day open to all. The team reasons that added transparency to the process will encourage participation not only from known leaders, but also new and emerging leaders — those with a keen interest in the school and its future, and those who will be ultimately responsible for implementing the plan.

In its all-call approach, the team invites prospective participants to pre-register. In order for participants to be prepared to do their best work at the planning session, the planning team prepares pre-registration strategic information packets for their review before visioning day.

Included in the participants' pre-registration packets are:
- Core values and/or core values statements;
- The school's mission statement;
- Strategic issues: a description of the most important issues facing the school

over the upcoming one to five years;

- White papers from administrators on how strategic issues impact their departments or divisions;
- Pertinent background readings chosen to shed more light on strategic issues;
- Relevant research results, environmental and internal, that led to the identification of critical issues;
- The visioning day's agenda;
- Desired outcomes of the day;
- Definitions of planning terms; and
- The strategic planning process outline.

With the help of the pre-registration list, the planning team creates breakout groups in advance, in order to bring together people with varying perspectives, backgrounds, and school roles, and to balance group dynamics. Known leadership is distributed throughout the groups, and each group serves as a microcosm of a cross-section of constituencies, which are interdivisional, interdisciplinary, and intergenerational.

In thinking about group composition, the planning team considers important tactical decisions. It decides that, rather than pre-appoint group facilitators, it will allow them to self-select. It also decides that planning team members will not be assigned to a group, but will serve as overall facilitators, keeping the groups on the task.

What do they talk about?
By giving everyone the same strategic information in the pre-registration packet as a starting point for discussion, the team is confident that informed conversations will develop, where intuitive thinking and opinion are challenged or confirmed by strategic information.

Planning day exercises are designed to create a shared vision, goals to achieve it, and strategies to move the goals forward. Resolution of the strategic issues, as indicated by situational analysis and environmental scanning, is important. There are several ways to frame strategic issues for processing. The team chooses to use open-ended discussion questions, and it challenges the breakout groups to return with their vision crystallized into a statement that they believe is a compelling word picture of the school's future success. As time allows, they may construct a vision narrative.

The team distributes a participant workbook at the onsite check-in to set the tone and keep sessions on track. In it are ground rules, roles and responsibilities, and details of the specific exercises that will be used in the visioning, goal-setting, and strategy sessions that day.

Developing a shared vision

During the planning day, breakout groups work independently on the visioning exercise in the participant workbook. They discuss, in light of the strategic issues that the school faces, such questions as:

- "What do we want to be true of the graduates of our school during and after their experience here?"
- "What is the most important thing for us to accomplish in the next three to five years?"
- "What does success look like for us three to five years from now?"
- "What do we want to be and be known as in three to five years?"

At the end of the allotted time, they reconvene in plenary session.

Narrowing down the choices

With a dozen breakout groups returning to present their own version of the desired future, the planning team explains that it needs a tool to help the group arrive at consensus. It has chosen "dotmocracy" as a voting tool to narrow the choices. A limited number of colored adhesive coding dots are distributed to participants, who are instructed to vote for the three vision statements that they identify with most. Because, in this case, there are 12 groups with 12 vision statements, and participants are given just three dots, their votes reveal each person's top 25 percent.

The team answers all questions: Yes, they may vote for their own vision statement. No, they may not place more than one vote on the same statement. No, dots may not be bartered or sold!

Each planning team member is given his or her allotted dots and votes with the others before the results are tabulated. The two or three vision statements that receive the highest number of votes form the basis of the next session, which is goal-setting.

The strategic planning team counts votes, transcribes, and distributes copies of the top vision statement(s) to the breakout groups as the basis for that session.

Goal Setting

The first decision each breakout group makes in this session is which vision statements they wish to work with. They record their choice and follow the directions in their participant workbook for goal setting. Groups work to answer the question, "What four to six major accomplishments will cause us to achieve this vision?" At the end of the allotted time, the groups return to the plenary session and report on their goals. Participants receive more adhesive coding dots and vote for the draft goals that resonate most with them.

At the end of the day, work sessions yield:
- One to three draft visions that generate substantial agreement;
- Dozens of draft goals through which run several recurring themes;
- A series of draft strategies to support draft goals.

Next steps

Activities for the strategic planning team will center on compiling and analyzing the visioning day's output. Dividing into work groups, one group will work on refining the vision based on the top draft vision statements, while another group tabulates and organizes the draft goals by theme. Within a few days, the planning team may release an early summary report to the campus community with a final draft vision statement, which invites review and comments.

Once comments are returned and reviewed, the final version of the vision statement will drop into place as a cornerstone of the strategic plan. Work will continue on sorting and refining the vision-driven draft goals. Alternatively, the planning team may decide against sharing the draft versions of vision and goals in favor of distributing the final board-approved versions later in the process.

SETTING GOALS IS A
collaborative
EFFORT

8 DETERMINING GOALS, STRATEGIES, AND INITIATIVES

By Christina Drouin, Founder and Executive Director, Center for Strategic Planning

Once you have identified your school's core values, mission, major issues, and vision, you will be ready to create your strategic plan. That process has three steps. You should:

- Identify your goals or the overarching achievements that will accomplish the vision;
- Determine your strategies or the various ways that you will achieve each goal; and
- Chart your initiatives or the specific projects, programs, and activities that will accomplish each goal.

Experts in strategic planning differ on whether you need to create a written document of those goals, strategies, and initiatives, and how extensive and complex it should be. However, most believe that at least some form of written record, even if it is brief, should be developed to ensure that all your key constituencies have something to reference as they go about their daily activities. That way, everyone will know that they are literally "on the same page" when it comes to the direction that your school hopes to take and what it hopes to achieve.

SETTING GOALS THAT BRIDGE THE GAP

People who work at independent schools set goals every day. Working toward student outcomes that demonstrate changes in awareness, knowledge, skills, attitude, behavior, and condition are the heart of the independent school's educational enterprise. Just as you create goals in the classroom and with extracurricular activities to stimulate student progress, you must create goals in strategic planning for your school to define the accomplishments that will lead you to your ideal future.

The purpose of defining goals is to determine the four to six major accomplishments that will help your school achieve its vision. When drafting each goal, you should ask:

- Is each goal consistent with our core values and mission?
- When each goal is reached, what will we see? Will there be significant change in awareness, knowledge, ability, skill, attitude, behavior, or condition?
- When each goal is reached, what particular element of the vision will be fulfilled? Is the goal necessary to fulfill the vision?
- Is each goal feasible given the current rate of performance and resources available? What are the gaps?
- When all the goals are reached, will the vision be realized?
- How will we measure each goal?
- Are we willing to be accountable for each goal?

To answer those questions, your planning team may want to perform a gap analysis. In a gap analysis, team members should ask themselves: "If this is what we stand for (values), and this is our purpose (mission), and this is where we want to go (vision), what four to six major accomplishments will bridge the gap between where we are today and our envisioned future?" They should also ask, "Of the resources we need to reach this goal, which do we have and which must we acquire?"

Your goals should be congruent with your institution's values and mission so that actions are aligned with beliefs. They should resolve your strategic issues and lead to the accomplishment of your vision. If you have used the Appreciative Inquiry approach described in Chapter 7, you would create goals that are built on your school's strengths. Instead of asking, "How can we solve our problems?," you would consider, "How can we strengthen what is most valuable about the school — and then use those strengths to address our problems?"

Setting goals is a collaborative effort involving people throughout the school and, at times, alumni, community leaders, and others. Overarching goals give people in all disciplines, divisions, teams, and other groups the chance to see themselves as contributing in their own areas to some aspect of your school's vision.

As a result, you should strive to establish goals that are understandable and meaningful. When goals have clear outcomes, all the people involved will know how to measure their success and be accountable for achieving those desired outcomes.

FRAMING YOUR GOALS

Although everyone can agree that goals are something to be achieved, opinions may vary about how they should be expressed. Some people prefer goals to be written in specific quantitative language; others choose to write goals in broad qualitative terms and accompany them with detailed performance measures.

What's important is to agree on a common approach and stick to it. If you decide to develop broad goals, which most schools do, your performance outcomes can be stated separately to bring together the qualitative and the quantitative.

People also have different views as to whether goals should be presented as activity-based or outcome-based. If you express a goal in terms of action, it is activity-based. Examples are "to recruit and retain quality faculty members" or "to seek and maintain a board of trustees of talent, commitment, and generosity." If the goal is expressed as the results your school wants to see when the goal is accomplished, it is outcome-based.

For instance, in its 2006-2010 strategic plan, Saint Mary's School, a day and boarding school for girls in grades 9 through 12 in Raleigh, NC, framed an educational excellence goal in terms of its desired outcome: "Saint Mary's School will be and be known as an exemplary school of academic excellence, spiritual growth, inclusivity, and character formation in the tradition of Episcopal schools." Your team can also develop outcome-based goals from activities-based goals by simply asking the question, "What will we see when this goal is accomplished?"

To reach its vision for 2007-2008 — "To be a model educational community committed to the individual learning styles of students" — McLean School of Maryland, a K-12 coeducational day school in Potomac, MD, developed the following goals:

- Enhance our focus on a student-centered approach to teaching and learning;
- Commit to a quality faculty that supports the vision, mission, and values of McLean;
- Sustain dynamic partnerships among all of McLean's constituents;
- Acquire the financial resources to secure the present and to respond to future growth and development;
- Seek and maintain facilities that are adequate in size and configuration to sustain and enhance our educational community and goals; and
- Create a community of learners.

Perkins School for the Blind in Watertown, MA, describes the goals it will pursue to reach its vision for 2010, which is to continue in its role "as a world leader in education for people who are blind, or deafblind…to impart hope and foster independence:

- Prepare our students to have the skills for a changing and competitive environment;

- Reach babies, students, and elders who are not receiving adequate services;

- Expand internationally; and

- Build partnerships with advocates, donors, and volunteers.

Ultimately, your school should develop its own specific goals and approach to framing them based on your particular values and mission, strategic issues and vision, and strengths and opportunities. Your institutional goals should be developed during a planning process that allows people throughout the school community to express their ideas, either at the formal planning workshop or through other forums, such as one-on-one discussions or meetings with various constituencies. Then, the planning committee should refine those ideas before presenting them to your board for final approval.

DRAWING STRATEGY FROM GOALS

Once you have put your goals in place, you must develop your strategies — those major approaches that you will take to accomplish those goals. As educators, school administrators and faculty members think in terms of learning strategies all the time. Crafting strategies to reach the goals of your plan is similar to crafting educational strategies. You ask yourself the same question: How can we do this?

Like goals, strategies can be gathered from the wider school community and reviewed, refined, and coordinated with your administration or the strategic planning team. To help identify four to six broad directional approaches or strategies, your school should test each one by asking:

- Is this strategy consistent with our core values, mission, and guiding principles?

- Does it describe a broad directional approach?

- Does it answer the question: How will we reach this goal?

- Does it help us make critical decisions about allocation of resources?

- Together, are all the strategies sufficient to reach the goal?

Strategies are action-oriented. When writing them, you should use active verbs that point toward a major direction. For example, to reach a goal of attracting the best students, you should use verbs such as target, segment, pursue, add, collaborate, and communicate. To create a community of learners, you should use verbs such as build, nurture, encourage, cultivate, and evaluate.

Recall the educational excellence goal of Saint Mary's School, described in the previous section. To reach that goal, the school identified the following strategies, among others:

- Pursue academic excellence with programs that meet the needs and develop the talents of all students;
- Create an environment that stimulates intellectual curiosity, independent thinking, and creative problem-solving, and that treats learning as a lifelong endeavor;
- Empower students to develop strength of character and provide them the means to understand the foundations of a spiritual and ethical life;
- Establish a climate of mutual trust, acceptance, and respect; and
- Help each girl identify her gifts, discover ways to develop them, and give them expression.

Typically, your school would retain the same strategies for the duration of your plan, although you should reevaluate them annually in response to changing conditions. You also should be careful to stay above the tactical level when developing strategies. Only after you determine the broad directional approaches indicated by your strategies will you be ready to identify the tactics, or the initiatives, that support each one.

ALIGNING INITIATIVES WITH STRATEGIES

When it comes to carrying out the details of a plan, who does it better than an independent school teacher? The same mechanisms that achieve desired classroom outcomes can be used to make your school's strategic plan a reality. Specific initiatives, such as projects, programs, and activities, are the engines behind the strategies through which you obtain your goals.

When Saint Andrew's School in southeast Florida launched a five-year strategic plan in 2000, that plan contained 185 initiatives. By 2004, more than 90 percent of those initiatives had been completed. The few that remained dealt with programming that would be put in place following a nearly completed facilities construction project.

None of the three previous strategic plans had been as successful in getting off the shelf and into action. Why? Because developing the plan to the initiative level gave everyone in the school community the chance to participate in developing tactics that would eventually lead to achieving the school's vision. Most important, everyone developed a real sense of ownership in the process and its outcomes. Writing initiatives at the divisional, departmental, and work-group levels allows those responsible for the future to shape it together in the present.

The key question that your school must ask itself in order to develop successful initiatives is: If this is what success looks like for us (vision), and this is what we must achieve to reach it (goals), and this is how we will achieve those goals (strategies), then what specific projects, programs, and activities will help us reach each goal and ultimately actualize our vision?

When developing your specific initiatives, you should also ask:

- Is this initiative consistent with our core values and mission?
- Does the initiative support the strategic plan in driving daily operations?
- Is this a change initiative that signals progress or improvement and not simply the maintenance of the status quo?
- Can we accomplish this initiative within the time frame of the plan?
- Can we write a work plan to accomplish this initiative?
- Can performance outcomes be written for this initiative?
- Do we know or can we identify the costs of this initiative?

To return to the example of McLean School of Maryland, one of its key goals was to "enhance our focus on a student-centered approach to learning." One strategy for reaching that goal was "to sustain and enhance a challenging curriculum that educates and prepares students for college and other future experiences." To carry out that strategy, the school identified 20 initiatives, including the following:

- Publish a curriculum guide for each division that will be updated yearly by the department chairs in conjunction with the administrative team;
- Find or create a learning-style inventory for use throughout the school and make students more aware of their learning styles;
- Sustain our current work in identifying learning styles with a more comprehensive look at identification and articulation of learning styles by students;
- Encourage students to use techniques to adapt information to fit their own learning style;
- Expand technology use in the classroom and curriculum;
- Enhance teaching strategies and techniques through ongoing professional development;

- Investigate and publish a study-skills and strategies guide and offer a summer course for prospective upper-school students to learn these techniques.

WRITING THE PLAN

People who argue against written strategic plans say that they are often large tomes that sit on the shelf, while the school goes about business as usual. But a written plan provides many important advantages. Stephen C. Carey, president of Association Management and Marketing Resources, indicates in the *Association and Nonprofit Strategic Planning and Research Guide,* "Many…senior executives and volunteers like to keep the strategic plan locked 'in their heads' or, as consultants like to say, 'in a drawer or on a shelf somewhere.' Oftentimes the leadership of the staff and the board certainly know where the organization is going but fail to write it down or articulate it or connect it with the ongoing work plan of the organization. By doing so, they do a disservice to the stakeholder community by not ensuring that the organization has a comprehensive plan that has been openly prepared, and to which all stakeholder segments have had an opportunity to contribute."

Your school might consider holding group-writing sessions organized by division, department, and committee (including board committees, parent committees, and student groups, as well as administrative leadership teams) or by strategic goal. That process can also be done online. Using a standardized initiative-writing template, individuals and planning units can consider what they can do to advance the school's vision, and they can identify and suggest projects, programs, and activities to be considered for inclusion in the plan.

As your school builds an inventory of those proposed actions, you should track the sources of the initiatives and supporting ideas and give them some priority. You can accomplish that by devising a simple ranking system and having the sponsor group code each initiative with a number, symbol, or color that has some meaning of priority. Once the planning team collects and reviews the initiatives, it should place all those that will be included in the plan under the appropriate goal and number them sequentially. Note that sequential numbering simply allows for easy tracking, monitoring, and reporting of progress on an initiative; it does not inherently indicate prioritization.

While the entire school should contribute to the plan, it is most efficient to select one or two people from your planning team to organize all the different pieces and write the final product. The author of the plan could be a trustee, the school head, or a member of the planning committee who has been delegated the responsibility. Before that person begins to write, you should choose the format for the plan and determine how extensive the written plan should be.

DIFFERENT FORMATS

In *Strategic Planning for Nonprofit Organizations* (second edition, John Wiley & Sons, 2005), Michael Allison and Jude Kaye distinguish three types of plans: the abbreviated, moderate, and extensive. In the abbreviated plan, the writer or writers "use notes from the planning workshop and summarize the key ideas on paper," the authors explain. "The key to writing the plan is to keep it simple and short, circulate it among internal stakeholders for their comments, and then submit the final version to the board of directors for approval." With or without a vision statement, an abbreviated plan might include a statement of the issues, goals, and corresponding strategies.

In the moderate version of the plan, the writers would provide more background information on the issues that the school faces and outline in some detail the goals and strategies, perhaps with a sampling of initiatives. The plan also would include an introduction from the board chair or the head of the school and appendices containing the results of external scanning and internal evaluations.

The extensive plan would include the initiatives developed by all departments and groups throughout the school, as outlined in the previous section. Each planning unit — individuals, departments, divisions, leadership teams, committees, or other groups — would be responsible for developing the initiatives. Then, the prime writer or writers would incorporate those initiatives into the strategic planning document. An extensive plan could include board-directed strategic thrusts over the first couple of years of the plan, as well as a description of your implementation strategy. Your implementation strategy should include naming the people who will be responsible for overseeing implementation, how you plan to prioritize initiatives and track and monitor progress, your feedback loops for exchanging information, and your approach to ongoing strategic thinking to keep your plan on target.

As Allison and Kaye note, however, "The rule of thumb for writing the extensive strategic plan is the same rule for writing the abbreviated strategic plan: Keep it simple and as short as you can and still provide enough guidance to develop an annual operating plan. The heart of the strategic planning document is the core strategies and program and administrative priorities/goals and objectives sections." In each of these three versions of the plan, you should include your school's core ideology of values and mission as a reminder of what anchors your institution, even as it stretches and grows into a strategic plan.

There is no one-size-fits-all method when it comes to publishing and distributing your strategic plan. You even can combine the abbreviated, moderate, or extensive versions with other communication tools and take a targeted approach. The point is to increase awareness and understanding of your plan, develop constituency commitment, and ultimately inspire action.

To accomplish this, you would develop a communications plan to accompany your strategic plan in which you list your key audiences, what response you desire from each, the best tool to elicit that response, in what venue, and when it should be accomplished. A broad array of communications vehicles is needed for such an approach. In addition to the print versions described above, they can include PowerPoint presentations; a list of talking points that you regularly incorporate into speeches and discussions; a brochure; vision posters; a one-page summary of values, vision, and goals; strategic plan pages on the school website; and interactive online feedback loops to help track and measure success.

Most important, your communication rubric should include a working document that presents at a glance how people throughout the school will carry out your strategic plan. It should be a fully integrated implementation plan that includes goals, strategies, and initiative-tracking columns for specific sponsors; targeted implementation years; budget needs; and status updates.

As Peter Drucker reminded us in *The Practice of Management* (reissued edition, HarperCollins, 1993), "The best plan is only a plan, that is, good intentions, unless it degenerates into work. The distinction that marks a plan capable of producing results is the commitment of key people to work on specific tasks. The test of a plan is whether management actually commits resources to actions which will produce results in the future. Unless such commitment is made, there are only promises and hopes, but no plan."

Your effort to implement your strategic plan's initiatives is the engine that drives the conversations needed to get your plan off the shelf and into action.

ESTABLISHING SUCCESS MEASURES

It's important to establish in advance the measurement devices that will eventually demonstrate that the strategic plan is proceeding successfully. Goals in a strategic plan can be measured in several ways:

By the completion of initiatives planned to meet them

When building a strategic plan based on a hierarchy of visions, goals, strategies, and initiatives, the completion of initiatives is one of the plan's built-in measurement tools. First, the four to six strategic goals, each and together, must be sufficient to realize the vision. Then, because you have crafted strategies for each goal, the goals eventually will be realized, as you carry out those strategies through specific projects, programs, and activities. Finally, goals become self-fulfilling as strategic initiatives progress. A board member once expressed it this way: "If reaching vision is like getting a touchdown, completing initiatives is the way you move the team toward the goal posts." By simply completing the initiatives that make up the tactical part of the plan, the school moves the team forward to the ultimate goal, which is the vision.

By quantifiable outcomes associated with each goal

In a strategic plan, goals easily can be broad statements of accomplishment, while performance outcomes can fit neatly under them as quantifiable outcomes-based measurements of change. For example, in its 2002-2007 strategic plan, the Hill School set as its goal for alumni, parent relations, and communications that the school will recognize "the importance of its constituencies and will aggressively pursue meaningful efforts to build relationships, solicit gifts at all levels, and steward donors."

To meet that goal, the school identified, among others, the following quantifiable outcomes:

- Secure gifts in all categories for all purposes to reach a total of $83 million or more.
- Solicit gifts totaling $5.5 million for phase 1 of the hockey rink construction and gifts of $4.5 million for phase 2 of the hockey rink construction.
- Begin construction of physical projects only when 50 percent of required funds are in hand and the remaining 50 percent in pledges will be received by completion of the project.

By dashboard indicators (pre-established quantifiable markers that can be periodically checked)

What will you see when the goal is accomplished? What changes in knowledge, abilities, skills, attitudes, awareness, behavior, or condition will give evidence that the goal has been reached? What are the markers along the way?

Setting a series of dashboard indicators to track the progress of each overarching goal gives a concrete framework for evaluation. Using this approach, the

The Language of Strategy

Here is some language that shows direction to help craft strategy:

Improve	Focus	Develop	Restore
Sustain	Differentiate	Innovate	Continue
Invest	Diversify	Adapt	Relocate
Mentor	Fund	Reinforce	Expand
Attract	Lead	Reward	Practice
Facilitate	Collaborate	Recognize	Integrate
Partner	Equip	Identify	Compete
Provide	Communicate	Reduce	Serve
Train	Build	Review	Retain
Enhance	Evaluate	Measure	Foster
Strengthen	Establish	Reclaim	Ensure
Research	Nurture	Institutionalize	Prepare
Enable	Learn	Position	Promote
Add	Teach	Discontinue	Create
Increase	Broaden	Implement	Change
Decrease	Encourage	Reconstitute	
Pursue	Cultivate	Revitalize	

— *Adapted from Frank Martinelli,* Strategic Planning Manual *(Center for Nonprofit Leadership, 1999)*

school should identify what must happen for each goal to be reached. Then it should tie performance measures to those critical elements of success, identifying what it will accept as evidence that they have been accomplished.

For example, if you are using the balanced scorecard method that The Forbes Group has recommended, you will want to evaluate how your school is performing before and after your strategic planning process based on metrics in the following areas: financial measures, customer-satisfaction measures, process measures, and skills and knowledge measures. Bruce Butterfield, The Forbes Group's president, has said that "the Achilles heel of strategic planning is implementation and measurement." He observes, "Without translating strategic direction into a program of work, a plan is meaningless. This is why it is imperative to link strategic and operational plans through indicators of metrics."

The McClelland School, a PS-8 co-educational day school in Pueblo, CO, has done just that by establishing a set of dashboard indicators for each of the goals in its current strategic plan. Here are two of the goals and their respective performance measures:

Program: McClelland School strives to offer a strong, college preparatory curriculum that builds on a continuum of skills from preschool through eighth grade. The program at McClelland is designed to educate the whole child and inspire lifelong learning in an atmosphere that promotes intellectual growth, creative expression, physical development, and a sense of responsibility and connection to fellow students and the broader community.

Dashboard Measures

- Accreditation
- Benchmarking best practices
- Test scores
- Participation in regional academic competitions and exhibitions
- Community service projects/contests/events
- Graduate tracking
- Parent perception/satisfaction

Faculty recruitment and retention: The McClelland School will attract and retain outstanding and dedicated faculty of diverse backgrounds and complementary talents. McClelland seeks faculty who will be excellent teachers and role models for students, who are committed to grow professionally, and who will contribute to the overall life of the school.

Dashboard Measures

- Recruitment and retention statistics
- Years of teaching experience
- Professional certifications
- Professional development opportunities/budget
- Comparative salary and benefit data
- Involvement with school activities, clubs, and events
- Customer satisfaction

Mark H. Moore has offered additional metrics for consideration in his working paper entitled "The Public Value Scorecard: A Rejoinder and an Alternative to 'Strategic Performance Measurement and Management in Non-Profit Organizations' by Robert Kaplan," published in May 2003 by the Hauser Center for Nonprofit Organizations at Harvard University. Moore suggests performance measures uniquely suited to nonprofit organizations in each of the following broad areas:

- The public value produced by the organization — the extent to which it achieves its mission, the benefits it delivers to clients, and the social outcomes it achieves.
- The legitimacy and support enjoyed by the organization — the extent to which "authorizers" and "contributors" beyond those who benefit

from the organization remain willing to license and support the enterprise.

■ The operational capacity the nonprofit organization is relying on to achieve its results. This includes not only measures of organizational output, but also of organizational efficiency and fiscal integrity. It also includes measures of staff morale and capacity, and the quality of the working relationships with partner organizations. And, it includes the capacity of the organization to learn and adapt and innovate over time.

IN CONCLUSION

The core of your strategic plan will be the goals, strategies, and initiatives that you develop to reach your vision. Goals are broad overarching statements of what your school must achieve to bridge the gap between its current situation and the future you envision. Your goals can be quantitative or qualitative, action-based or outcome-based.

Strategies are statements of the major approaches that will be used to attain your goals; they describe a general approach, not specific activities or projects. Initiatives are the projects, programs, and activities, prioritized annually, which must be accomplished to achieve your stated goals. Individuals, departments, teams, committees, and other groups are the sponsors of initiatives and responsible for their advancement. Performance outcomes are specific, measurable statements of what changes in knowledge, awareness, attitude, skills, behavior, or condition are sought. Dashboard indicators for each goal can help track your plan's progress.

The success of today's strategic plans is determined by the effectiveness of their implementation and their flexibility in course correction. It becomes easy to achieve, track, monitor, and report accomplishments if you properly set goals, action-oriented strategies, specific initiatives with clear success measures, timelines for implementation, assignment of responsibility, and have champions among the school's top administrators.

Some people worry about getting lost in the details of dozens of strategic initiatives and losing the big picture. How can your school guard against the plan becoming just another set of tasks to fulfill and criteria to meet? The answer lies in the continual reinforcement of the connection between the daily tactical work of initiatives, on the one hand, and the broad strategic direction of the school, on the other. The challenge for school leaders is to keep the school's vision and strategic thrust ever-present during each stage of the plan.

ADDITIONAL
MATERIALS

The Relationship Among Goals, Performance Outcomes, and Indicators

The following matrix of two goals gives some examples of the relationship between goals, performance outcomes, and indicators:

Goal	Performance Outcome (or measure)	Indicators
Goal 1: Create a new and cohesive K-12 academic program.	**1.1** By the end of 2001-02, current curriculum delivery will meet the goals of the stated K-12 curriculum	**1.1** Curricular maps **1.1** Increased department area supervision from department chairs
	1.2 By the end of 2001-02 the use of technology will be integrated into the daily life of the school	**1.2** Greater use of technology in coursework (i.e. teaching, planning, homework, assessment) **1.2** Use of website by both faculty and families for academic information
Goal 2: Assess current academic faculty, staff, and administrative evaluation processes and establish processes where they do not currently exist	**2.1** Understand and implement supervised goal setting to advance strategic initiatives of the school	**2.1** Formal goal products with evaluations **2.1** Documented evidence of periodic conferences between department chair and employee

Being Where You Want To Be

Now that you have your plan, how can you put it to use most effectively? Lawrence Sykoff, head of Ranney School in Tinton Falls, NJ, outlines in the final section of this book how to carry out your plan and keep it relevant, despite unexpected changes along the way. He describes how you can:

- Communicate the plan to people inside and outside the school so that they will be eager to implement it;

- Make your plan work with your operational and financial plans;

- Avoid common pitfalls;

- Reassess and recalibrate the plan in response to changing circumstances; and

- Ensure the plan remains vital and contributes to the school and its future.

Section **IV**

""HAVE A
destination
IN MIND

9 MAKING YOUR STRATEGIC PLAN WORK FOR YOU

By Lawrence Sykoff, Head of School, Ranney School

The last thing that you want is to have your strategic plan just sit on a shelf. Once your planning committee has developed it, and your board of trustees has signed off, you will need to involve people in the process of carrying it out.

During the early stages of the plan's implementation, you will be in a good position to garner the support of the entire school community, as well as interested people outside of your school, so that they fully understand and appreciate the outcomes that the plan is designed to achieve. People will demonstrate more support and buy-in for the plan after you have educated them about its benefits. Therefore, to manage effectively your strategic planning process during the rollout phase, you will want to communicate often about the unfolding of your plan to a wide variety of stakeholders. You will need to provide frequent, focused, and specific information about its goals and action steps.

COMMUNICATING ABOUT THE PLAN

Your school's head is usually in the best position to arrange both formal and informal meetings with representatives from your various constituencies to present and discuss the strategic plan. He or she should remind people why your school undertook the strategic planning process, let them know how the new plan will affect them, highlight any major changes and why those changes are occurring, and explain how each person will play a role in helping make the plan a reality. Such gatherings should provide a sense of openness and an atmosphere of full disclosure about your new strategic goals. In such conversations, your school head and other institutional leaders will have the opportunity to illuminate the strengths of the plan and how it will ultimately improve the quality of the educational experience for current and future generations.

Depending on their circumstances, priorities, and the goals of their plans, schools differ as to which groups are their most important constituencies. As Christina Drouin, founder and executive director of the Center for Strategic Planning, has observed, "When it comes to sharing the plan with others, it's easy to be conservative and cost-conscious, limiting your distribution to board members, administrators, current families, and key donors. But think of the missed opportunities." She notes, "A strategic plan anchored in values and mission is a compelling relationship-building tool with a wide range of publics, markets, and individuals who have both direct and indirect potential impact on the school's attainment of its vision."

To make sure that you haven't overlooked a key group and the best way to reach it, you should consider developing a communications matrix that charts by audience your desired outcomes and the best choice of communications tools. You should identify the key groups at your school, and consider developing different versions of the strategic plan for each audience that you target. For example, you might want to give some audiences just the executive summary, others a one-page summary sheet, and others the entire document. You also should develop different ways to tell each constituency about the plan and to involve them in it. In addition to face-to-face meetings, you also might consider newsletters, strategic planning news releases, and dedicated space on your school's website.

For example, Saint Mary's School in Raleigh, NC, launched its strategic plan, "SMS 2010: Imagine That!" with a festive celebration. Faculty members, administrators, staff, students, parents, alumnae, and current and past board members attended. A spokesperson for each goal built enthusiasm for the plan by naming specific items within that goal that he or she viewed as particularly exciting or significant. Administrators distributed a printed version of the plan to everyone present and also placed the plan in faculty and staff members' mailboxes. The administration followed that by sending a more detailed brochure version of the plan — containing vision, goals, and strategies — to all of its key constituents.

Just as important, the communications didn't stop with the kickoff. The head of Saint Mary's continues to describe the plan in presentations to constituencies both on and off the campus, including at alumnae gatherings. A different staff person highlights an aspect of the plan at every monthly faculty-staff meeting. The strategic plan drives each board agenda. In addition, a short electronic version of the SMS 2010 is available on the school's website, and the full version is downloadable. Values, mission, vision, and goals are posted around campus. The Saint Mary's administration routinely includes the plan in admission packets and with donor materials. The school also uses the plan in faculty recruitment and hiring as well as in board cultivation, recruitment, and orientation.

If your school is a relatively large institution, you may also want to create a special newsletter about the details of the plan for people outside your direct school community. Local residents, community leaders, and others will appreciate your interest in keeping them abreast of emerging activities. The establishment of community partnerships can be quite valuable, particularly if you plan to construct new facilities. New classroom buildings often create more traffic issues; expanded athletics fields and spectator seating areas may generate more noise. Your school's leaders should anticipate neighbors' concerns and communicate with them in a timely manner to ease or alleviate any negative reactions.

For example, you might host town meetings on campus with neighborhood residents, send information about the strategic plan to the community newsletter, speak at civic associations or service clubs, and invite local business leaders to the school for a breakfast, luncheon, or evening background session. In some cases, inviting local politicians to the school to view architectural renderings and learn about major school-wide strategic initiatives firsthand can provide them with a script about the plan, because they often are called upon to speak before community gatherings and field important questions about your school and any expansion plans. Dealing with difficult questions at informal school gatherings can often head off controversy or contentious debate that might otherwise occur at municipal hearings and other venues less within your control.

In sum, organizations and individuals within and outside your school are more apt to be supportive of your plan if, along the way, they have been asked to provide their ideas and opinions. Moreover, communicating and disseminating information about a new strategic plan offers your school's leaders the opportunity to reaffirm your institutional mission and articulate an evolving vision. The strength of any strategic plan resides in its ability to enliven the school community with enthusiasm about how new strategic goals and action plans can sustain reverence for your school's established ideals, while also creating new opportunities for everyone.

INVOLVING PEOPLE IN CARRYING OUT THE PLAN

Depending on the size and scope of the plan, some schools engage an army of people to carry out their strategic plan, while others involve a small,

Whom Should You Inform about the Results of Your Strategic Planning Process?

Past, current, incoming, and prospective board members

Those with shared responsibility for implementation, especially current faculty members, administrators, and staff members;

People outside the school who participated in planning days, workshops, focus groups, or peer reviews

Current, incoming, and prospective students

Current, incoming, and prospective parents

Alumni

Parents of alumni

Grandparents

Current and prospective donors, foundations, and other funding groups

Incoming and prospective faculty members, administrators, and staff members

Accrediting associations

Professional membership associations

Educational consultants

Feeder schools

Colleges and universities

Licensing agencies

City and county governments, planning boards

Professional colleagues

Peer institutions

The greater community

— *Christina Drouin, founder and executive director, Center for Strategic Planning, www.planonline.org.*

representative sample of different constituency groups. Whatever the case, your teachers, administrators, and staff members can provide an invaluable reservoir of potential talent and expertise during the implementation stage. You should consider creating implementation committees that include a mix of representatives from those groups.

One of the key roles of such committees is to bring the plan alive on a daily basis. You will want various departments and units within your school to use the strategic plan as a guide and to develop specific programs and activities that contribute to your institution's overall goals. Everyone on those newly formed committees should understand their role and purpose in the process so they should, therefore, receive a proper orientation from the board of trustees and planning committee.

You may want to form implementation committees that are aligned with the strategic plan's major areas: academic initiatives, student activities and advisory systems, financial aid, diversity, facilities, and so on. An alternative would be to align them with the plan's key strategic goals. As such, the scope of your strategic plan will dictate how many committees you will need to monitor action plans.

Often the school's management team is a group that should lead the committees, as those leaders are usually up-to-date with the strategic plan's evolution and progress. The use of division heads, business managers, and development officers as team leaders or co-leaders can be very effective in helping manage complex issues and questions. For instance, at Ranney School, where I serve as head, we train key administrators to take leadership roles on various planning committees, such as retention and attrition, marketing and branding, and site-plan development.

You can also assign leadership of the implementation committees to a veteran vanguard — people on the staff who have institutional history and the poise and confidence to value a variety of opinions, appreciate and manage lively discussions, and remain focused on the action plans. Generally, the architects of the strategic plan — the specific people assigned to develop the goals and action steps — also should maintain an active role in carrying out the plan. That will serve to sustain a sense of continuity from the plan's creation through its implementation. For example, the strategic plan for McLean School in Potomac, MD, titled "Linking Today with Tomorrow," gained traction by having the divisions, departments, teams, and other groups who would be responsible write their own initiatives — more than 140 in all — to support the school's key goals. By actively involving trustees, faculty members, and administrators in writing the plan at the tactical level, the school increased the likelihood that efforts to carry out the plan would be successful.

You should also at least consider recruiting people from outside the school — those individuals who can add value but are not directly affected by the plan's outcomes — to serve on the committees. For example, a local architect, educational leader, business professional, lawyer, accountant, or landscape architect can provide unbiased expertise, because he or she does not have a personal stake in the immediate results of the school's initiatives. The involvement of outside members on implementation committees is another way to foster positive communications and goodwill in the community where your school resides.

MAKING YOUR PLAN WORK WITH YOUR OPERATIONAL PLANS AND GOALS

In *Strategic Planning for Nonprofit Organizations* (second edition, John Wiley & Sons, 2005), Michael Allison and Jude Kaye use the metaphor of driving your car while on vacation to describe the need to align your strategic plan with your school's daily operations. "It is important to have a destination in mind, your long-range goal. The destination alone, however, is not enough to get you there successfully," they write. "You need to have detailed information about which roads are most likely to get you there, estimates about the distance to be covered and the time it will take, estimates of how much money will be needed for meals and gas for the car, and warning systems to tell you if the engine gets overheated or other systems fail."

"Now imagine that you are not driving the car alone. Instead you have 20 people doing different jobs simultaneously," Allison and Kaye continue. "This is the stuff of annual operating plans and budgets: Which programs and management/operations functions are going to be implemented in the upcoming year, by whom, by when, and how much 'gas' (money and person power) will they require?"

Your operating plan should be the basic outline of the steps that you will take to begin carrying out your strategic plan and, as such, it should be congruent with the priorities that you've outlined. In the ideal situation, your school's head and management team, after discussions with teachers, administrators, and staff members, will produce an annual set of goals that deal with all the important areas of your school. Many of those annual goals can be completed in relatively short periods of time, whereas strategic goals will take longer to implement. Still, your strategic goals generally should be an outgrowth of your annual operational goals, and your annual operating goals should, in turn, help you carry out your strategic goals.

To get McLean School of Maryland's strategic plan off the shelf and into action, for example, the head of school formed an interdisciplinary K-12 implementation team with responsibility for prioritizing, monitoring, reporting, and evaluating plan performance. At the end of each school year, the team identifies the following year's strategic initiatives based on the priorities that the board of trustees identified at the launch of the plan. Members of the implementation team act as liaisons for each of the targeted annual initiatives. They meet each month to anticipate issues and unlock logjams, and they deliver progress reports to the board, faculty, and administration each year.

Charlotte Latin School in North Carolina officially launched its strategic plan, "Great Expectations," in March 2004. The head appointed an implementation team, consisting of teachers and administrators from the school's three divisions, to monitor the timeline and completion of the 194 initiatives contained in the plan. Approximately 30 to 40 initiatives were scheduled to be accomplished annually in support of the plan's six major goals. That team is responsible for selecting each year's initiatives and works directly with the teachers and parent organizations of the school to assure continuity and consistency between the operational plan and the strategic plan.

Many schools use summer planning retreats to review the progress of the past year and identify new goals and ways to obtain them for the upcoming year. An outgrowth of such annual planning often produces a list of blue-sky needs or a wish list that your trustees will need to further review and discuss. The refurbishing of old facilities, the building of new facilities, the addition of parking spaces, and the establishment of an academic endowment to support special programs can evolve from annual operational goal-setting that reinforces and strengthens your strategic plan. For example, our management team at Ranney annually evaluates the school's accomplishments in a variety of different areas — teaching and learning strategies, enrollment, marketing, development — and provides trustees with reports of our progress towards strategic goals. Through that process, we unfetter the board from micromanagement and help it stay focused on larger institutional issues, long-term planning, and governance.

Moreover, annual planning by itself has broad value. In such meetings or retreats, the head and the management team can enhance their working dynamics and coalesce on the relevant issues. Such activity provides a focal point for the team as it develops new tactical strategies to reach key goals.

DEVELOPING A FINANCIAL PLAN TO GO WITH THE STRATEGIC PLAN

Institutions, like individuals, have many lofty goals and ideas that often outreach their financial potential to realize them. Your school's leaders should maintain a practical financial plan that marshals resources for immediate needs while, at the same time, providing a growing base of support for the anticipated requirements of future generations of students and families.

Three Questions to Ask as You Implement Your Strategic Plan

1. What new skills will board and staff members need to successfully implement the strategic plan?

2. How might current structures and systems...need to change in order to support the new vision?

3. How might the organization's culture (mindset) need to change to support new core strategies?

— *Michael Kaye and Jude Allison,* Strategic Planning for Nonprofit Organizations *(second edition, John Wiley & Sons, 2005)*

At Charlotte Latin School, for instance, the administration and the finance committee of the board annually set aside money from the operating budget to support the strategic initiatives planned for the upcoming school year. This process began a year before the development of the strategic plan, when funds were earmarked for consultant fees and other expenses associated with the plan's development. The school adds more resources to the annual budget each year based on the specific initiatives that the administration chooses, and the board approves, from the plan.

Sound financial planning sometimes will require the leaders of your school to make hard decisions, always recognizing the difference between a need and a want, about what projects and programs the institution can or cannot pursue at certain times. The 2001 action plan of Sidwell Friends School, in the Washington, DC, area, put it this way: "[P]riorities inevitably involve choices, which invariably mean difficult tradeoffs among worthy but at times competing needs...Short-term needs may have to go unaddressed while critically important long-term challenges receive priority." For example, through its planning process, Sidwell Friends decided to delay construction of additional facilities until it had increased its endowment and raised faculty salaries. Once those challenges were addressed, the school enthusiastically committed resources to its delayed facilities priority.

A financial plan that is developed specifically to support a strategic plan should take into account school policies that govern debt-service limitations and capital fund-raising requirements. Some schools use a variety of financial-planning strategies, combining robust capital campaigns with some borrowing from endowment, commercial banks, or state-bonding agencies. Many schools also keep up an active annual fund drive during a capital campaign so they do not compromise current operational needs. In such cases, communication of those dual fund-raising activities generally requires frequent discussions with supporting constituencies.

The development of a strong and substantive financial plan, one that supports an emerging strategic plan, should be a continuing process. Anticipated revenue can be forecasted and even generated, if you establish targeted financial goals. Moreover, your school head and trustees regularly should engage in a process of longer-term financial forecasting. That will require developing, and reviewing every few years, a *multi-year* financial plan that accounts for salaries and benefits, facilities management, tuition levels, endowment growth, financial aid, and other ancillary programs.

Through such effort, it will become clear what programs your school can financially support — especially potentially large programs that require sizable amounts of revenue. If your financial plan is built on such a strong foundation, it will serve to enhance growth, protect against downturns in the economy, and provide for unanticipated situations.

ESTABLISHING A LONG-TERM STRATEGIC PLANNING COUNCIL

In almost every instance, the final stages of a strategic plan require periodic input from the community. Each school, depending on size and culture, generally has an effective mechanism to manage such communications. If you handle feedback properly, your school will continue to grow and evolve, even amidst some criticism and dissenting opinions. Criticism is inevitable, but if your plan is clear and focused, that criticism can be clear and focused as well. A good strategic plan helps make criticism constructive.

Although the board of trustees usually is charged with managing your school's overall plan, and school administrators are responsible for any midcourse corrections to it, an experienced board and school head never will underestimate the potential for advice and feedback that exists in the community. Your school should continue to ask teachers, administrators, alumni, parents, and others — people who think strategically — for their counsel and recommendations. For example, parents with a history at the school, those people who have committed to the long term for their children, are excellent resources, when you are in need of truthful and straightforward input. Their advice has considerable value, because their perspective is informed, and they want to see your school continue to excel.

One good way to tap such expertise and judgment is to establish a long-term

What Questions Are Most on People's Minds?

in Brief Every person who hears or reads about the planning process should be able to answer each of the following questions:

- Where are we headed and when will we arrive? (Vision)

- Why are we headed there? (Strategic imperatives or issues)

- What will we see as we change? (Goals)

- How will we engineer the change? (Strategies)

- How specifically can I be involved? (Initiatives)

- What won't change? (Values and mission)

— *Christina Drouin, founder and executive director, Center for Strategic Planning,* www.planonline.org.

strategic planning council. An oversight group has many advantages, the most important of which is to provide a formal structure to assess the strategic plan's progress. The council, which also can include the chairs of the implementation committees or other stakeholders, has the responsibility to gather data from a variety of sources, to determine whether the plan is on track, and to send recommendations to the board. The board can, in turn, submit essential questions to the council about the effectiveness of the plan in meeting your school's priorities.

WHY SOME PLANS FAIL IN THE IMPLEMENTATION STAGE

There are several common reasons that some plans fail during the implementation stage. You will want to avoid:

- Poor communication;

- Distracted leadership and administration;

- Lack of financial resources;

- Inadequate training and professional development;

- Stakeholder buyout; and

- Shrinking enthusiasm and commitment from the school head or the board of trustees.

Of course, on the most fundamental level, you will have the best chance of success in carrying out your plan if you have managed the initial phases of your strategic planning process well — when your school's leaders convinced people of the advantages that a new order of life would produce. Experience tells us that people need to make sense out of change and truly come to believe that innovative planning will improve the current state of affairs. Oftentimes, making sure that your constituencies understand the intent of change from the very beginning is as important as the change itself.

In addition, schools can be very emotional, fragile environments and susceptible to resistance when routine and habit are interrupted. Strategic planners can make the mistake of believing that new must be better, and sometimes find it difficult to empathize with opinions to the contrary. Building a new future, therefore, also will require you to build a new consensus.

The challenge for your school's leadership in this process is to take the time to listen, but to remain fiercely engaged in seeing the plan succeed. Inevitably, major school undertakings like a strategic plan have positive results when leadership maintains perspective, holds steady, and manages and deals with the occasional conflict.

IN CONCLUSION

The success of a strategic plan is enhanced and assured when there is sustained:

- Oversight;
- Communication;
- Dedication and passion to succeed;
- Open and honest discussion;
- Flexibility, yet an unwavering commitment to the plan's priorities;
- Focus and involved school leadership — with enough understanding to be supportive, innovative, and even uncompromising when it comes to being the keepers of the dream;
- Resources, human as well as financial, to make the plan a reality; and
- Support and involvement from the board of trustees.

Most of all, the success of your school's strategic plan will be determined at the outset, when the plan is a natural outgrowth of the institution's major priorities and requirements. Those priorities that most reflect and emulate the fundamental values of your school's mission are generally the ones most worthy of pursuit in a strategic planning process.

Ultimately, if you properly evaluate and carry out your strategic planning process, you will reach a successful conclusion, culminating in a celebration of everyone's efforts to see the plan reach fruition. This kind of a result can produce broad-based confidence in the school and generate feelings of accomplishment among all your key constituencies. It will demonstrate to the community the value of preparation, planning, perseverance, and teamwork.

10 BECOMING A STRATEGIC-THINKING ORGANIZATION

By Lawrence Sykoff, Head of School, Ranney School

Astrategic plan rarely marches to the finish line without at least a few complications along the way — it is a "plan," not a gospel. Good school leadership requires regular intervention and innovation, and your school's head, in consultation and coordination with the implementation committees, the long-term council, the board of trustees, and others, should understand and anticipate that a strategic plan periodically needs alteration.

Typically, as suggested in the last chapter, a designated implementation committee or the long-term planning council should revisit your strategic plan each year to determine if the larger priorities of the plan remain in alignment with your school's annual operational priorities. No matter how well you have planned, the old saw "Nothing is quite as sure as change" certainly applies to the strategic-planning and "strategy-making" process.

REASSESSING AND RECALIBRATING THE PLAN IN RESPONSE TO CHANGING CIRCUMSTANCES

Shifting circumstances — sluggish donor support, underestimated expansion costs, changes in school leadership, internal school conflicts, board turnover, fluctuations in the economy, unusual enrollment patterns, and many others — can influence how you carry out your strategic plan. A strategic plan may also need revisiting because the original plan was too ambitious or not inclusive enough of major school priorities. With the help of an active steering committee or long-term council, you can make adjustments in a timely and effective way.

For example, in the 1990s, the country experienced swings in economic growth, which affected all sectors of the economy, including private schools. During that volatile period, the strategic planning process for the development of the middle-school and upper-school buildings at Ranney School, where I serve as head, was underway. As a result, we changed our plan to place a greater emphasis on student retention than school recruitment. We felt that if the school was strong internally, attrition would diminish — which would relieve the stress of trying to recruit new families when they had less discretionary income to pay for independent education.

That change in the strategic plan proved to be quite significant because it placed emphasis on shoring up deficiencies with better programs, stronger staffing, and more capable management. In the long run, that recalibration of the plan reshaped the school, which led not only to a successful capital program, but also enduring and sustained educational value. Indeed, our school had its strongest era of growth during one of the most difficult economic cycles in the last decade.

Another case in point: After more than two years of plan implementation — which resulted in the completion of nearly 70 percent of its 185 strategic initiatives — Academy at the Lakes in Land O'Lakes, FL, took a step back. It re-evaluated the extent to which its plan, "Charting our Course," was still on target. The executive-leadership team reexamined the vision and goals of the plan and determined that the major work that had been done in building its program and stabilizing enrollment had set the stage for a forceful push toward the finish line. The team assessed its current external environment by surfacing issues and writing assumptions. Then it turned its attention to building alternative future scenarios that addressed such issues and assumptions in the context of its strategic plan. The team presented those scenarios to a work group of the board for further discussion and debate. The result has been a sonar-like focus on what needs to be accomplished for the remainder of the school's current planning cycle.

THE IMPORTANCE OF "RED FLAG" MECHANISMS

If ignored, some changing conditions can ultimately become troublesome. Thus, your school head and board of trustees should establish "red flag" mechanisms that will sound an alarm if the plan encounters any problems. For example, you should:

- Review key benchmarks. In the best of all worlds, you will have already established such benchmarks or dashboard indicators when you wrote the plan. (See Chapter 8.) For example, Sidwell Friends School has identified a number of key measures to assess the school's progress and general health, and its administrators and trustees review them regularly. Some of those benchmarks include measures of student retention, student and faculty diversity, faculty and staff compensation, and other key areas. (For more in-depth information about Sidwell Friends and its planning process, please see the "Case Histories" in the following section.)

- Examine the effect that new strategic plans have had on the attitudes of the staff through regular formal surveys or focus groups.

- Conduct systematic meetings with the key people who were targeted to receive the most benefit from a particular strategic initiative. For instance, new buildings will produce reactions from students and parents, while new academic programs will generate responses from teachers and administrators.

You should also continue to review the process or procedures used to inform the staff and administration about the benefits and advantages of new strategic innovations. Quite often in the strategic planning process, so much attention is devoted to the idea of a brighter future that the practical issue of training and professional development, which is needed to bridge the gap between the pres-

Key Steps in Implementing and Recalibrating the Plan

- Identify overall plan priorities or strategic thrusts;

- Appoint an implementation team or teams;

- Develop an implementation plan with feedback loops;

- Communicate the implementation plan throughout the campus community;

- Assign roles and responsibilities;

- Set annual priorities, including budgetary requirements;

- Implement priorities;

- Establish a tracking and evaluation system with feedback loops;

- Track and evaluate results;

- Share lessons learned;

- Acknowledge successes through frequent and open communication;

- Continuously scan both internal and external environments for new and relevant strategic information;

- Regularly test the plan's underlying assumptions against new information.

— *Christina Drouin, founder and executive director, Center for Strategic Planning*
  www.planonline.org

ent and the future, is ignored. You will need to revisit the planning process under such circumstances and provide the staff with sufficient training.

As you modify your strategic plan, you may also need to:

- Discuss the change and gain approval from the board of trustees.
- Communicate with committees about the mitigating factors requiring a midstream change in direction.
- Announce to the school community the reason and rationale for altering the existing plan. For many schools, a periodic strategic plan newsletter is an appropriate venue for communicating changes or modifications to the original plan.

It is also important to note that, however buffeted by change your school may be, you should only make changes to your strategic plan with the end result in mind: the larger institutional dream. You should not succumb to internal or external pressures to make major or significant alterations to the plan that will redirect institutional priorities. In fact, the more the plan is guided by the school's fundamental vision statement, the less that you will need to make changes.

SUSTAINING MOMENTUM

Independent schools are changing all the time. New teachers bring divergent pedagogical ideas, more families on campus require enhanced communications, a larger enrollment requires more financial support, on and on. The normal rhythms of a school are always resonating with the elements of change.

However, planned change is different. The exercise of influence by your board of trustees through a formal set of recommended institutional innovations *demands* people to change — and that is where the tension begins. For example, capital-expansion programs often require people to move their environments, learn new teaching technologies, teach more students, and attend more meetings. In a very real sense, people are asked to leave their comfort zones.

Clearly, such change is periodically needed to reinvigorate the organization. But such change can be difficult and, therefore, must be placed in a context in which people can understand — especially if they are going to embrace the innovation and make it work. As such, your school leaders must make a concerted effort to build and sustain consensus around anticipated change.

As part of that effort, you should also report progress to the school community. In the words of Christina Drouin of the Center for Strategic Planning, "Progress toward vision should be communicated and celebrated. Lessons

Questions to keep in mind for monitoring the success of your plan

The planning committee should organize and plan a yearly retreat that would focus on these questions:

■ Is the current strategic plan on target? What has or has not been accomplished?

■ Are the assumptions of the internal and external environment still valid?

■ What are the current issues facing the organization, and, after discussing these issues, do any changing or new priorities need to be added to the strategic plan?

■ Are there any new performance targets and/or modified intermediate checkpoints that need to be looked at?

— *Michael Allison and Jude Kaye,* Strategic Planning for Nonprofit Organizations *(second edition, John Wiley & Sons, 2005)*

learned should be shared. The implementation team should report to the campus community with regular progress reports to keep momentum and enthusiasm high. Newsletter and Web updates, all-school events, faculty meetings, parents' receptions, and the like are all excellent opportunities to keep people connected to the plan and its progress."

Such regular "show them the future" communications, with good visual displays, can serve to maintain broad-based enthusiasm and support among your school's various stakeholders. Demonstrating a positive vision through your plan's evolution will remove angst and concern. Such communications can also become a catalyst for future strategic planning activities.

During such periods, your school's leaders will have the unique opportunity to recall for the community the values they are supporting. It is an exceptional chance to build strong relationships. Thus, revisiting your plan so that you adopt an ongoing, nimble strategic posture has many supplementary benefits beyond that of the plan itself.

IN CONCLUSION

When people understand and support the idea that strategy-making and its resulting planning documents can enhance your school on both a personal and institutional level, the learning curve for everyone reaches new heights. Under such circumstances, your school will become dynamic and evolve with integrity and purpose. The greatest outcome from such periods of institutional advancement is the understanding of, and the appreciation for, the true value strategy-making offers as a *constant and unending* process. Your school will become a strategic thinking institution—one that meets its goals and thrives, regardless of unanticipated occurrences and influences.

Indeed, a successful strategy-making process can have a transforming value for your school: the potential to improve the quality of life for all. The energy from a well-designed and comprehensive strategic plan can electrify and galvanize your school community around a common purpose. If developed and administered effectively, it can ignite a seminal period of growth and renewal, ensuring that your school becomes and remains the institution that you and the rest of the school community have always dreamed that it would be.

ADDITIONAL
MATERIALS

Inside the Strategy Box — Recalibrating Strategy

One approach to ongoing strategic thinking is the disciplined assessment of what did work, what is working, and what might work in the future given what was, is, and might be important in seven major domains of strategy: governance, mission and identity, organizational development, product and service development and delivery, constituency and market development, competition, and finances.

You can base your assessment on three critical factors at work in each of the seven areas:

1. The future relevance of current assumptions;
2. What you have previously identified as important;
3. What you pinpoint might be important in the future.

Areas marked by important changes in opportunities, threats, strengths, and weaknesses call for rethinking and recalibrating previous strategy choices.

The following matrices provide a process tool for strategic thinking. To complete a thorough examination, complete these steps for each of the seven domains.

1. To complete the "Was" column, ask: "What was important in this area, what was our vision of success, what was our corresponding strategy, and did it work? What were our assumptions about the future?"
2. To complete the "Is" column, ask: "What is important in this area, what is our vision of success, what is our corresponding strategy, and is it working? What are our assumptions about the future?"
3. To complete the "Might Be" column, ask: "What might be important in this area, what might be our vision of success, and what might be our prevailing strategy? What might be our assumptions about the future?"

Governance

Governance	Was	Is	Might Be
Important			
Vision			
Strategy			
Assumption(s)			

Mission/Identity

Mission/Identity	Was	Is	Might Be
Important			
Vision			
Strategy			
Assumption(s)			

Organizational Development

Organizational Development	Was	Is	Might Be
Important			
Vision			
Strategy			
Assumption(s)			

Product and Service Development and Delivery

Product & Service Development & Delivery	Was	Is	Might Be
Important			
Vision			
Strategy			
Assumption(s)			

Constituent and Market Development

Constituency & Market Development	Was	Is	Might Be
Important			
Vision			
Strategy			
Assumption(s)			

Competition

Competition	Was	Is	Might Be
Important			
Vision			
Strategy			
Assumption(s)			

Finances

Finances	Was	Is	Might Be
Important			
Vision			
Strategy			
Assumption(s)			

Case Histories

In the following section, you will find case studies of how three schools developed their strategic plans and are making them work on an continuing basis.

- Sidwell Friends School in Washington, DC;

- St. Paul's Episcopal School in Oakland, CA; and

- Ranney School in Tinton Falls, NJ

Section V

Case History I

SIDWELL FRIENDS SCHOOL
Washington, DC

In 1998, Sidwell Friends School, a pre-K-12 day school in the Washington, DC, area, engaged in a comprehensive evaluation of what it should do to support its fundamental values and, at the same time, deal with its most crucial needs for the future. That process began at the same time as the appointment of a new head of the school, Bruce Stewart. According to Stewart, the key responsibility of the leader of an independent school is to vision what the school will need to be effective two or three decades hence: "What do the kids who are in school right now need to know so that they can be successful in 2030 and beyond?"

Sidwell Friends has long had a broad-based commitment to offering a challenging curriculum and a vigorous learning environment grounded in the Quaker values of personal integrity, service to others, respect for individual differences, and community consensus. Its other core values are uncommon personal and academic excellence, the prizing of diversity, and environmental stewardship. The school's top administrators and the board of trustees had concluded that certain policy changes were needed to enable the school to sustain and enhance those values, reflect on future priorities, and carry out its mission in a world of rapid change.

PLANNING THE PLAN

As a first step in building its strategic plan, the board established a planning committee made up of trustees and several key administrators. "When we put the committee together, we asked ourselves, 'What kind of qualities and traits do we need?'" recalls Stewart. "For example, we determined that the head of development and the head of business operations should both serve on the committee, because they would have to help raise the money, manage the funds, implement the plan's goals, and articulate those goals to others."

To gather additional perspectives, Sidwell Friends also established an advisory board to guide the head of school. It was made up of alumni, former trustees, and other long-time friends of the school with extensive experience in education, business and finance, philanthropy, medicine, technology, and communications. When Stewart or various committee members needed special expertise, they contacted, on an ad hoc basis, specific people at Sidwell Friends or in the broader community who had such expertise.

As the planning committee embarked on its work, it asked itself the following questions:

- What societal forces will most impact Sidwell Friends in the years immediately ahead?
- What physical plant, equipment, and financial resources will be needed to fulfill the school's mission over the next decade?
- How should the school's identity as a Quaker institution influence the balancing of its educational priorities?
- What are the implications of the school's current dependency on tuition revenue?

In answering those questions, the team drew on a number of earlier studies and policy reviews, including the school's 1986 diversity report, a 1993 alumni association task-force report, a 1996 self-study leading to re-accreditation, and the work that the school recently had done to define what it sought in a new school head.

The committee determined that the school was, in many ways, in as strong a position as it ever had been in terms of its applications, acceptance ratios, student retention, diversity initiatives, and many other measures. Yet it was also clear that a number of major societal trends also would impact the school in the very near future in significant ways. Those trends included:

- Significant population growth in the region;
- Growing dissatisfaction among local families with public education;
- A projected dramatic increase in teacher retirements over the next decade;
- Rising technology costs;
- An accelerating globalization of the economy; and
- Competition among independent schools for faculties and facilities that would serve to increase, not reduce, costs.

Much of the planning work involved how to deal with those trends and ensure that the school would thrive in the future.

The planning committee's efforts also were informed by an extensive process of consultation with parents, faculty, staff, students, alumni, neighborhood residents, and other members of the larger Sidwell Friends community. "The head of the school, with the support of the trustees, should set the school's vision, but the plan also must be fully inclusive and have the buy-in of the entire community," notes Stewart. "People need to feel informed, appreciated, and that they have real ownership. That way, a school will develop a plan that everyone supports."

To that end, Sidwell Friends hosted a number of open forums with key stakeholders to discuss the issues confronting the community and how the plan should address them. The school ensured that it held several meetings at different times and places, so that everyone who was interested in learning about and contributing to the plan could attend.

"At that point, we had more of an outline than a fully formed plan. The public sessions helped us on the board and in the administration flesh it out," Stewart explains. "We would listen carefully to what people said, and if they made good suggestions, which they often did, we recognized that we had to address those points and incorporate them into the vision or revise it accordingly."

"For instance, I went to the high school student body and presented the plan," he recalls. "And the kids would ask things like, 'Mr. Stewart, how much is that going to raise my tuition?' And I went back to the board and said, 'We have to be careful that we don't create a debt service that we can't sustain without raising tuition 8 percent instead of 6 percent. What's a healthy balance? Where is the golden mean?'"

Stewart continues: "We had all those feedback mechanisms working all the time — and continue to do so. We are always watching, listening, and thinking about whether this is the right way to go."

DEVELOPING AND CARRYING OUT THE PLAN

After evaluating the data that it had gathered and the input that it had received from a wide range of Sidwell Friends constituencies, the committee identified the following policies and practices as most requiring attention:

- Endowment growth;
- Faculty compensation and support for professional development;
- Curricular and co-curricular innovation;
- Tuition and fee setting;
- Financial aid growth;
- Physical plant and equipment sufficiency.

And it established the following priorities and goals:

■ Raise the school's endowment principal by $10 million, not including market appreciation, to support salary growth and tuition assistance.

■ Revise the faculty compensation system to sustain the school's ability to recruit, retain, reward, and renew a faculty of the highest national caliber.

■ Identify and support additional programs of continuing education and professional development for faculty members, using a "Venture Grants" program to encourage faculty development of new courses, innovative teaching approaches, creative uses of technology, and the understanding of other cultures.

■ Readjust tuition levels to eliminate the current tuition differential between the lower and middle and upper schools over the course of several years — with appropriate financial aid support for those students and families most impacted by the changes.

■ Give clear attention to adeptly balancing institutional investment in "bricks and brains" to ensure a capable and highly motivated faculty and student body along with full sufficiency in facilities and cutting-edge teaching equipment and materials.

Sidwell Friends administrators and trustees also developed strategies and initiatives to carry out its goals, working through the school's committee structure. That began with the school's administrative council, on which the top 11 administrators sit, including the principals of the lower, middle, and upper schools; the development director; the finance director; the admissions director; the diversity coordinator; and others. The school also worked through various faculty committees. For example, the academic policy committee dealt with the academic life of the school, which took the lead in implementing changes in the plan that related to curricular matters. A special compensation committee spearheaded work on issues concerning faculty and staff pay and benefits, and so forth.

Stewart describes how he, as the school head, has approached implementation of the plan. "First, I take the four values of the school and our key objectives in the plan and ask, for example, 'If we are committed to uncommon academic excellence, how do we know if we are succeeding?'" He focuses on what he calls the four "P"s: program (curricular and co-curricular), personnel (employees and students), plant, and pecuniary matters.

■ *Program:* "What do we need to do with our curriculum? In the case of science, for example, how can we take kids beyond the classroom and science lab and help them to learn by involvement with application and discovery?"

- *Personnel:* "How do we continuously recruit, retain, reward, and renew vital and talented faculty and staff?"

- *Plant:* "If we want to get and keep first-rate science teachers, SFS must have first-rate science labs and classrooms, strong technology, and innovative equipment like SMART boards" — electronic white boards with computer capabilities and applications (manufactured by SMART Technologies). "Five or 10 years ago, teachers wouldn't have raised the issue, but it's a different day now. I need good labs to get good teachers."

- *Pecuniary matters:* "All the prior 'P's require a significant measure of financial investment. What will they cost? What can we afford? What is the best source of funding? What can't we afford not to do?"

That approach to each major objective has helped significantly to guide the process of implementing the school's vision.

GAUGING THE PLAN'S PROGRESS

By the end of fiscal year 2005, Sidwell Friends' endowment had doubled in size from the 2000 level. Faculty salaries were increased, so that they were competitive with those at other national and local peer schools. A Venture Grant program made about $100,000 available annually for faculty grants and a nearly similar sum for continuing education. Also, the school created a special loan program to help employees buy homes.

Meanwhile, by the beginning of 2002, progress on the strategic plan's goals was so well along that the trustees and Stewart began to address the need for upgraded and new facilities. The school conducted a facilities needs assessment, working with a broad range of constituencies, including faculty and staff, trustees, parents, students, alumni, and consultants. By November 2002, the board had determined that the school required what was then thought to be $34 million worth of new building and improvement projects. A $56-million capital campaign was launched to further increase endowment and support significant construction and operating expenses on the school's two campuses. To date, the school has raised more than $40 million, and based on such progress, the campaign leadership expects to meet the full goal.

To measure the school's success in achieving that goal and others, Sidwell Friends' board requires the administration to conduct annual benchmarking of how the school compares to its peer institutions. The benchmarks include student/faculty ratios, admissions profiles, the provision of financial aid, student and faculty diversity, faculty and staff compensation, capital and annual fund raising, and such other measures as the board may deem valuable from time to time in assessing the school's general health and mission.

In fact, at the beginning of every board meeting, the trustees focus on different data points. "The board constantly reminds me that the plural of anecdote is data," Stewart says. "We ask ourselves questions like, 'How many people are on scholarship?' 'What is the average grant?' If our goal is to have one in five students on financial aid, and the number begins drifting downward, a flag would go up. We would wonder if that was a trend. We would know that we need to monitor that area much more closely. Either we weren't using our financial aid resources wisely, or we weren't getting the pool of candidates that we'd like."

"We are looking for the data points that help us connect and correct. Yet at the same time, we realize that not everything that counts can be measured, and not everything that can be measured counts," he adds. "There are things that you simply can't benchmark and nail down. Instead, it's all about intuitive judgment. We try to keep a balance between the two approaches."

REVISITING THE PLAN

In response to changing conditions, Sidwell Friends continues to revise and recalibrate its plan. As Sidwell's action plan states: "Any long-range plan, if rigidly adhered to, will have unintended and perhaps untoward effects. Good governance requires that this plan be closely monitored by the administration and the board and adjustments made if necessary to uphold the school's educational mission."

"The rate of change is constantly escalating, and the moment the ink is dry, you have to start making modifications," Stewart observes. "We've watched construction costs go up nearly 20 percent in our city over the last few years. Instead of local spending declining after September 11, it has ramped up. The growth of people coming into our area has been huge. That's been driving up construction costs, so we have to readjust the phasing of our building projects."

"For example, we may end up with three new buildings instead of five, or we may take a little longer to build all five," he continues. "Or we may do what is called value engineering. Early on, we made a decision that we want 'full sufficiency' in our facilities; in other words, we would never build a gym, say, without a shower. But we can get along with stainless steel rather than bronze facilities in a restroom. We can look at materials that can be environmentally responsible and attractive yet less expensive."

A strategic plan forces choices, but it ensures that those choices are thoughtful and intentional — that a school will not be buffeted about and pushed along at the mercy of unexpected circumstances. As Sidwell Friends' plan states: "Vital endowment requirements will need to be weighed against building projects; for instance, the desire to raise faculty and staff salaries and increase financial aid will need to be compared to the importance of moderating the rate of tuition increases….These tradeoffs require our community's understanding, that all things are not possible, and that we ultimately will define our school by our choices."

The chief benefit of good strategic planning is that a sound plan allows you to set a strong course and then be able to make wise tradeoffs if and when circumstances change. In fact, according to Stewart, a plan is, fundamentally, a direction. "Schools are not terribly different from huge modern oil tankers; it takes some time to turn them around but it can be done without beaching the craft — if the original plan is made with care and intelligent flexibility. A good strategic plan allows a school to set sail and yet to change directions when good judgment dictates."

And, finally, Stewart emphasizes the need to be constantly reassessing your position. "There's a moment when you have a focused dialogue and refine it and say 'Here's the plan.' But you know the world won't stand still for the next few years until you have another plan. What if construction costs change? What if the Federal Reserve raises interest rates? What if your campaign brings less than you hoped? You have to keep reassessing where you are. The best kind of strategic planning is a veritable movable feast. It is all-encompassing, all the time."

Written with the assistance of Bruce B. Stewart, Head of School, Sidwell Friends School

Case History II

ST. PAUL'S EPISCOPAL SCHOOL
Oakland, CA

I n 2000, when Karan Merry became head of St. Paul's Episcopal School in Oakland, CA, the school faced several key issues. Other schools with which St. Paul's competed for students were improving facilities and expanding classes. But while St. Paul's — a K-8 independent day school founded by the vestry of St. Paul's Episcopal Church — had wanted to do the same for most of the previous decade, the school had not been able to do so.

A study in 1990 had shown that having more students would better serve St. Paul's Episcopal School's mission and that the school would benefit from economies of scale of a larger school. Demand for St. Paul's education was high, and the space and other resources for a larger student body would allow the school to reach out to children from a wider range of backgrounds. In addition, with two more sections in each grade, the school would be able to rearrange class groups every year. Students would be able to have more interactions among themselves, which is a benefit to each child's social and emotional development.

The school's goal was to have at least 400 students enrolled and a minimum of two sections in each grade. After the 1990 study, St. Paul's added second sections in the sixth, seventh, and eighth grades and acquired several buildings. Yet the school was not able to get a capital campaign off the ground that would allow it to expand as it hoped. By the time Merry arrived as the school's head, it was confronting some critical facilities needs.

In the spring of 2001, the board initiated a strategic planning process, the first in St. Paul's history. This one-year effort involved numerous constituencies, led by an outside facilitator. At that time, most of the major issues of concern were evident, and in large part, the purpose of the plan was to organize and reinforce programs that the school had already identified or embarked upon. The board believed that the school needed a comprehensive strategic plan to support the school's direction. The focus was on process: buy-in from and discussion among the different constituencies. "The main objective was to gather different constituents together to take part in a conversation about the long-term vision of the school — to really examine the institution and reflect on its future," explains Merry. "In our case, those constituents were the church, board, administration, faculty, parents, and alumni."

THE PROCESS

In all, 21 people participated, including the board president, six other board members, a former board member, the head of the school, five administrators, four faculty members, and three parents. Two St. Paul's board members served as co-chairs of the strategic planning committee. The committee met monthly for a year and regularly informed the entire board of its deliberations and progress.

Vicki Larson, a St. Paul's Church parishioner serving on the board and strategic planning committee co-chair, commented on how the mission played an important role in the strategic planning process: "During the process, our focus on the mission of the school was the strong tie that bound us together. The school's core values became evident not only as we discussed them, but also as people passionately described their experiences coming to this unique community. Many times, I could feel the passion in the room as people told heartfelt stories describing how the school's philosophy had changed their lives (and their children's). Throughout our discussions, we reaffirmed the importance of the school's mission, and our collective commitment to it."

The board determined that the planning process needed an outside expert to provide guidance. The facilitator counseled the school on the initial research that needed to be completed before the strategic planning committee began its efforts, and he led each meeting and worked with the committee to develop goals and write the plan.

As an initial step, the strategic planning committee reviewed benchmark data, self-studies, and previous strategic plans. Some of the information dealt with salaries, tuition, and demographics. The division directors, as well as faculty members, often reported informally to the group.

After evaluating that information and discussing it among the group, the committee developed a plan that the board approved in April 2002. It included the following recommendations:

- Commence expansion of lower school;
- Address facilities needs;

■ Put the school on a sounder financial footing;

■ Consider adding a third middle school section to grades six through eight once the lower school expansion was complete.

In fall 2002, the board authorized commencing the lower school expansion of one class each year. To guide the board's decision, the administration developed a detailed financial statement to demonstrate the economic efficiencies of an expanded school and prepared scenarios of how the school would house students and operations in the current facilities. Later that year, St. Paul's hired an architectural firm to prepare a facilities master plan. A committee worked with the architects to produce a plan that addressed critical facilities' needs in the most cost-efficient manner.

To carry out the strategic plan goals, the school organized an implementation team, which included Merry and the directors of the lower school, the middle school, finance and operations, admissions, development, and administrative programs. The director of administrative programs was responsible for overseeing the plan's implementation. The team met several times during the 2003-2004 school year to create a document that established priorities and tasks, and identified the appropriate people to carry out the plan. The following year, the school integrated the strategic plan into its daily operations and used the planning document as its self-study action plan for the California Association of Independent Schools/Western Association Schools and Colleges.

By September 2004, the board approved a facilities plan that consisted of a renovation of one building, seismic work at another facility, and the construction of a new gym, playing field, and library. The school issued low-cost bonds and raised funds primarily from individuals and family foundations to expand the endowment and to pay for construction.

ACCOMPLISHMENTS

Thus far, the results of the strategic plan include:

Curricular and Co-Curricular Programs

The strategic plan didn't call for new programs, but instead outlined programs that the school wanted to maintain and improve. Throughout the expansion and major construction projects, the school maintained key services and activities, including a professional development and training institute for teachers, a curriculum review process, and an educational support model based on the Schools Attuned Program, which was developed by Mel Levine, a professor of pediatrics at the University of North Carolina Medical School in Chapel Hill, NC. Lastly, throughout the construction projects, the school provided resources and space to ensure that Aim High, a summer academic program for Oakland public and parochial school students, could continue to run its program.

Enrollment

St. Paul's expanded its enrollment in grades K-3 from one class to two classes at each grade level and expects to complete expansion of the fourth and fifth grades in two years. The board also approved the expansion of the sixth through eighth grades from two classes to three classes in each grade starting in 2009.

Facilities

The school retrofitted one building and renovated another. In March 2006, the board also voted to renovate a third building and utilize an adjacent property to construct a gym, a library, and a K-2 educational center, as well as expand the outdoor play space. This project will enable the school to create three discrete educational centers — K-2, 3-6, and 7-8 — to provide students with developmentally appropriate learning and play spaces.

Finances

The school created a 10-year financial plan and developed an annual process to review and update that document. St Paul's also initiated a capital campaign that is focused on building the school's endowment, while continuing to pay for construction projects through bond financing.

LESSONS

According to Merry, "It is important to document the plan because the process forces people to set concrete objectives for the next five years. The document lets people know about the direction of the school in a clear and concise manner. There is no confusion. Everything develops from the strategic plan."

She continues: "Developing a plan with the input of so many constituencies over a year-long conversation legitimizes many of the school's programs and future plans. As we have started our facilities upgrades and our enrollment expansion, we have been able to reference back to the strategic plan as a way to explain to people how we arrived at our decisions."

Another key lesson that St. Paul's board members and administrators say that they learned from the process is that once a school develops a strategic plan, the work has just begun. Integrating the goals of the plan into the daily operations of the school takes time and much conversation between and among the board and the administration. Further, members of the board and the administration change over the years, resulting in a group of individuals who are not familiar with the plan and the institutional rationale for and history of each strategic goal. They will continue to need to be educated about various aspects of the plan.

The final lesson that St. Paul's administrators highlight is that the strategic plan must stay relevant. Each year, at one of the two annual board retreats, school administrators and trustees examine key elements of the plan as a way to update it regularly.

In fact, in 2007, the school is coming close to the end of its five-year planning period. The trustees have asked the administration to analyze certain operational and environmental conditions to help the board make some key long-term decisions. The board also has set aside two planning retreats that will be facilitated by the same outside expert who guided the current strategic plan. The goal is to use the background information and the retreats as a way to develop a more comprehensive and refined process that will provide a regular assessment and update of the strategic plan.

In the words of Robert Davenport, president of the St. Paul's board of trustees, "Each year, we will focus on supporting our administration and faculty in the ongoing process of enhancing the learning experiences of our students. The primary vehicle for that support is a board-sponsored strategic assessment, combined with an initiative to update our existing five-year strategic plan — with provisions for annual refreshes — that will keep St. Paul's at the forefront of K-8 education."

Written by Josh Stern, Director of Administrative Programs, St. Paul's Episcopal School

Case History III

RANNEY SCHOOL

Tinton Falls, NJ

I n 1993, six years after the death of its charismatic founder, Russell Ranney, Ranney School found itself at a crossroads. Enrollment at the school had fallen, Mr. Ranney's successor and long-time assistant was about to retire, and any fund-raising capabilities were just emerging. At the same time, the school was struggling to manage two distinct campuses: the main campus and a satellite site some 20 miles away. Even as the board searched for new leadership, some trustees wondered how the school could reverse the negative enrollment trend and flourish.

Today Ranney operates a single 60-acre campus, enrollment is more than 800 and growing, the annual fund is running at about $350,000, and the development office is finishing a $14-million capital campaign, the second since 1999. New buildings and renovations feature state-of-the-art instructional technologies. The school enjoys a national reputation.

The administration and board of trustees at Ranney created such change by following the framework and many of the principles that James C. Collins presented in *Good to Great* (HarperCollins, 2001). Ranney's transformation, like those of Collins' model companies, took place through "disciplined people," "disciplined thought," and "disciplined action." Six key concepts characterized the changes that the school has used in its strategic plan to achieve great results:

Leadership motivated by a quest for excellence and an ambition for the organization to succeed. Independent schools subscribe to a set of core principles: values and character, high-quality teachers, and capable administration. With such qualities as a guide, the school's new head, Lawrence Sykoff, used every opportunity to speak to teachers, parents, alumni, trustees, and community members about the mission of independent education. In that way, the school began to realign itself with not only its own philosophical underpinnings but also those associated with dynamic institutions everywhere. Sykoff also determined, and communicated to people within and outside of the school, that educational quality had to be the overarching reason for all strategic decisions — that any change had to be inspired by a desire to improve the quality of the educational experience for each and every student.

—— **The honesty to confront the school's shortcomings while maintaining an unwavering path toward overcoming them.** In 1995, Ranney's board of trustees unanimously approved a detailed strategic plan with both short-term and long-term goals. The plan was visionary as well as practical; it sought to reshape the nature of the school, to discharge those traditions and practices that were no longer productive, and harness those that were still meaningful and viable. It took the school almost three years to fully integrate the nature of its new mission, which reflected the contemporary philosophy of knowledge, vision, and honor.

A single focus: academic excellence. From its inception, Ranney had been firmly committed to the basic tenets of a liberal arts education, providing students with rigorous course work. The school also had a demonstrated expertise in graduating exceptional scholars. Alumni often spoke about the fine education they received at Ranney School, and many of them became leaders in their professions. Thus, as the school started its "comeback," those central origins of academic quality — of presenting the region's finest academic program — were refortified.

A dogged commitment to the promotion of academic excellence in every arena. That commitment extended to athletics and the arts, and was also reflected in the school's willingness to shed programs that did not support this key area of excellence, or "hedgehog concept," as Jim Collins described it in *Good to Great*. For example, the school had to make a major decision to sell its satellite campus, which ultimately reduced the school's financial burdens — freeing up the resources needed to make long-overdue improvements on the main campus. Those additional resources also provided opportunities for investment in new programs, among them new sports teams; refurbished classrooms, art studios, and science labs; and additional elective and advanced placement courses in the upper school. With a downsizing of total school size, the main campus was able to flourish and reach enrollment levels today that have surpassed the highest enrollment numbers in the school's history.

"Looking back, we made difficult decisions with a gritty and resolute determination to do more with less — a fundamental and prudent business practice that, in this case, was aimed at one target: educational quality," recalls Sykoff. "In the end, the old adage, 'One has to take a step backwards in order to take two steps forward,' proved to be true."

The courage to make sweeping changes in personnel to secure the right people in the right positions. As Collins points out, for institutions to flourish and sustain distinction, "the right people must be on the bus and in the right seats." Strong leaders do not shrink from this assignment, as they know that it's most important to maintain personnel, especially administrators, who can effectively carry out the institutional mission and be the "keepers of the dream."

During the plan's implementation, some teachers and administrators retired, some decided the new school plans were not in alignment with their philosophy, and, in other cases, difficult personnel decisions were made as a result of a new performance review program. "While some personnel changes can be difficult and emotionally disturbing, a school's leadership must have the courage to create effective performance and review systems," Sykoff says. "It's important that the best teachers and administrators are rewarded and encouraged, and those who are weak be provided with clear professional development goals to retool or asked to move on. In institutions undergoing change, there is always a direct proportional correlation to the amount of change with the rate of turnover — the two are inseparable," he continues. "In fact, boards must appreciate this relationship and remain focused on the larger goals while supporting difficult administrative decisions."

Technological investments to enhance the quality of instruction and increase student achievement. For example, Ranney has invested in more than 60 SMART boards. The boards allow teachers to save board work to a linked laptop for future review, print notes from the board for class distribution, project images and information from the Internet that the students can study and work with, and much more. A new distance-learning auditorium, equipped with teleconferencing software and interactive cameras, provides students and teachers international access to programs, conferences, seminars, and classes all over the world. In addition, the new outdoor observatory and soon-to-be-installed in-school star lab will result in the development of the school-wide astronomy curriculum.

Even through the recession after September 11, 2001, which hit the New York metropolitan area particularly hard, Ranney School enjoyed sustained growth, financial stability, and success as a result of its strategic planning. Today, its strategic planning mindset continues to foster steady expansion and improvements in school programs.

"In this day of growing expectations for schools to perform well, with an ever-increasing requirement to provide high-quality educational experiences, it is essential for boards and school leaders to take every opportunity to be strategic with regard to future planning, " concludes Sykoff. "To be effective, strategic planning must be ongoing, and not reserved for special times. At Ranney School, we believe that the efficacy of our school today will determine the success of the next generation, and the future should never be determined by chance. Our children, and our society, are too important to do otherwise."

Written with the assistance of Lawrence Sykoff, Head of School, Ranney School

Sample Worksheets

You can use the following documents, or adaptations of them, to help you in your own strategic planning process. Except where noted, all are provided by Christina Drouin, founder and executive director, Center for Strategic Planning.

STRATEGIC PLANNING CHECKLIST

The basic strategic planning sequence can be broken down into a series of tasks, some of which appear in the lists below. They are organized by where they fall in the planning process. Responsibility for some of the tasks could be allocated to the strategic planning committee or its chair, while others are frequently handled by outside planning consultants. It is important to clarify early on in the process who — consultant or school — will be responsible for each of the tasks.

Preparing to Plan

❑ Form a strategic planning steering committee.

❑ Use the steering committee to develop a brief statement of the school's present strategic position (e.g., recently completed a successful $10-million capital campaign and building project, coming off of three consecutive years of declining enrollment in the lower school, anticipating the retirement of a successful long-term head of school, etc.).

❑ Hold conversations with several planning consultants about how they might work with the school.

❑ Select a planning consultant and agree on a scope of work (e.g., What role will the consultant play in the planning process?).

❑ Set a date for the strategic planning workshop.

❑ Determine list of invitees for the workshop.

❑ Issue invitations.

Collecting Data

❑ Collect dashboard indicators and benchmarks from StatsOnline for your school and its most salient competitors.

❑ Gather demographic data on your market.

❑ Summarize (or conduct) a constituent survey.

❑ Summarize any recent accreditation site visit reports.

❑ Hold telephone interviews and/or focus groups with key stakeholders.

❑ Select two or three relevant articles on the future of independent schools for reading by workshop participants.

Conducting the Workshop

❑ Clarify the facilitator's role and that of the steering committee and head of school.

❑ Examine the school's mission.

❑ Perform a SWOT analysis.

❑ Identify key issues based on this analysis.

❑ Develop a vision of a successful (ideal) future by addressing threats and capitalizing on opportunities.

❑ Articulate strategic directives and long-range goals, capturing sample implementation tactics as they arise.

❑ Prioritize directives for most immediate action.

Writing the Strategic Plan

❑ Create a writing team (four or five individuals from the workshop).

❑ Render flipchart pages and other notes from the workshop into a draft strategic plan.

❑ Review and edit the draft in multiple iterations.

❑ Create action plans and timelines, and assign responsibility for each long-range goal.

Approval and Roll-Out

❑ Steering committee submits plan to the full board for review and approval.

❑ Board approves plan.

❑ Prepare and publish an executive summary of the plan.

❑ Distribute copies of the executive summary to all constituents and post the plan on your school website.

❑ Hold informational meetings with faculty, staff, parents of students, alumni, and members of the local community to discuss the contents of the plan.

Evaluation and Monitoring

❑ Determine criteria for year-to-year evaluation of the strategic plan.

❑ Create a scorecard for periodic reporting to the school community.

❑ Assign responsibility for evaluation and monitoring of the plan to one individual or committee of the board.

— *Marc T. Frankel and Judith L. Schechtman, senior consultants and partners, Triangle Associates, www.ta-stl.com.*

SETTING THE PLANNING PARAMETERS

1. Why are you commissioning this strategic planning process? (To build community, to positively affect the future, to improve performance, to clarify mission, to correct major organizational issues, to strengthen alignment of beliefs and deeds, to position the school for ongoing strategic thinking, to help prioritize activities and focus your resources? Some of these? All of these?)

2. What planning horizon will you use? (Is this a three-year or five-year plan?)

3. What planning approach best fits the culture of your school?

4. When do you want this project to be completed and ready for implementation? (Is this a six-month, nine-month, or full-year project?)

5. How will the board of trustees be kept in the loop? Who from the team will report? What will be reported and when?

6. What planning elements, if any, will the board require signoff on beyond values, mission, vision, and goals?

7. Which of the following constituencies will be represented on the strategic planning team?

Board	Administrative leadership	Students
Parents	Faculty	Staff
Alumni	Founders	Other

STRATEGIC PLANNING TEAM: ATTRIBUTES OF THE PROJECT TEAM

Check for representation across groups:

❑ Board ❑ Parent ❑ Administration

❑ Faculty ❑ Staff ❑ Student

❑ Alumni ❑ Founders ❑ Other (example: divisional representation)

Candidate	Constituency	Group Representative	Visionary Thinker	Strategic Thinker	Known Research/ Analytical Skills	Opinion Influencer	Consensus Builder	Available to Serve

WINNING CAMPUS SUPPORT FOR THE STRATEGIC PLANNING PROCESS

Your board members, administrative leaders, faculty and staff members, parents, alumni, and students are core constituencies whose involvement in strategic planning will not only enrich your process but also significantly influence its results. You will want to engage them early and productively. To accomplish this, a communication plan that identifies audiences, key message points, communication tools, venues, and timeframe is a must. Most importantly, the head of school should take an active and visible role in delivering strategic planning messages.

Using a combination of written and electronic communications, small and large group sessions, and one-on-one meetings, you should fully brief your constituencies on why you are undertaking strategic planning *now*, your expected outcomes, their particular roles, and the benefits they will experience from the process. Overall campus support for your planning process will intensify as each audience comes away from each communication with a clear understanding of why, when, and how the process will unfold, and most importantly, how it positively affects them.

Some of the communication tools you might consider:
- Personal letters from the head of school
- Items in the school newsletter
- Items in the school magazine
- Informative e-mails
- A PowerPoint presentation about the strategic-planning process to be delivered at group meetings (faculty, board, parent, all-school)
- A page on your school website dedicated to strategic planning
- Regular progress updates through print media or Web postings
- Branding your plan with a name and visual identity for use every time you communicate about the plan

Presentation venues might include:
- All-school meetings
- Opening faculty meeting
- Divisional faculty meetings
- Board meetings
- Parent leadership groups
- Grade-level parent coffees
- One-on-one meetings with key leaders

- Student assemblies
- Off-campus presentations at community special events and alumni gatherings

Message content should include:

- Explanation of the benefits of strategic planning in general

- The rationale for strategic planning at your school

- The expected outcomes of this planning cycle at your school

- Orientation to your school's planning approach

- The particular role(s) of the constituency being addressed

- A draft timeline with milestone dates

- Names of the individuals who will manage the process

- Go-to people for questions and answers

- Invitation to participate (for example: in surveys, focus groups, community-planning day)

Communication Plan

Audience	Key message points	Desired outcome	Tool and/ or venue	When	Assigned	Status
Board of Trustees						
Administrative Leadership Team						
Faculty/Staff						
Students						
Parent Leadership Groups						
Parents						
Alumni Board						
Parents of Alumni						
Donors						

STRATEGIC ISSUES QUESTIONS FOR THE BOARD OF TRUSTEES

"The most common source of mistakes in management decisions is the emphasis on finding the right answer rather than the right question."
— Peter Drucker

In his book, *Crafting Strategy* (Measurement International, 2000), consultant and strategist Bob Frost states that strategy is about five things: setting direction, long-term success, competition, distinctive capabilities, and sustainable advantages. Strategy, he says, is about your plan for how you will achieve your ambitions and prevail over competitors and obstacles. Fundamental to successful strategic planning and its corresponding strategy design is asking and answering the right questions.

From Dr. Frost's book, here is a sampler of some essential questions that an independent school board of trustees would find provocative to discuss and debate as an exercise in strategic issues discernment. These questions could also be discussed by your school's administrative leadership team.

Questions about direction
- Are we in the right business for today?
- Are we in the right business for the future?
- Are we responding properly to emerging trends?
- What more should we be doing about emerging issues?

Questions about long-term success
- Do we have a vision of the future appropriate for an organization like ours?
- What is the long-term condition of our relationship with customers?
- Are our distinctive capabilities right for the future?
- Given our present capabilities, what portion of future opportunities can we expect to capture?
- On what basis do we prefer to compete in the future?
- What are our long-term prospects for creating value?

Questions about competition
- Is our basis of competition right for us? What might improve our basis of competition?
- Do we compete against the right competitors?
- How can we combine new competitive advantages or protections with those we already have?
- Must we improve operational effectiveness to protect ourselves from those

who are more efficient?
- Why are we better than others in creating value?
- How might our competitive position become unique?

Questions about distinctive capabilities
- What are our distinctive capabilities?
- Do our distinctive capabilities match our markets?
- What other markets are good matches for our distinctive capabilities?
- What is the longevity and future value of our intellectual property?
- What is unique about our people and their talents?
- What is unique about our business processes and practices and how they contribute value?

Questions about sustainable advantages
- How might our competitive advantages be made more sustainable?
- What new competitive advantages could we create or acquire that would be more sustainable?
- What could reduce or eliminate our competitive advantage? How might these events be prevented?
- How might we control the competitive game through industry standards and other points of leverage?

STRATEGIC PLANNING INTERNAL AND EXTERNAL RESEARCH TEMPLATE

	Sample	Method	Instrument/ Tool	When	Assigned	Done
Internal Scan						
Organizational						
External Scan						

THE STRATEGIC PROCESS

SAMPLE PARENT SURVEY

Parents with siblings, please complete a separate survey for each child.

Please circle ONE response. My child is a student in the:
A. Lower Division   **B.** Middle Division   **C.** Upper Division

Directions: Place a check mark (√) under the column that best rates your response to each question. Place your completed survey in the envelope provided, seal, and return to school by _____

1. In thinking about your expectations of a private school education for your student, how important a factor would you say each of the following characteristics was to you when you chose this school?

	Extremely Important	Very Important	Important	Somewhat Important	Not at all Important	No Opinion
College placement of graduates						
Academic rigor						
Faculty expertise						
Emphasis on student-centeredness						
Balanced learning environment						
State-of-the-art facilities						
School image in the community						
Diversity of campus population						
Emphasis on character education						
Emphasis on global consciousness						
Extracurricular opportunities						

2. How satisfied are you with each of the following attributes of education at this school as your child has experienced it?

	Extremely Important	Very Important	Important	Somewhat Important	Not at all Important	No Opinion
College placement of graduates						
Academic rigor						
Faculty expertise						
Emphasis on student-centeredness						
Balanced learning environment						
State-of-the-art facilities						
School image in the community						
Diversity of campus population						
Emphasis on character education						
Emphasis on global consciousness						
Extracurricular opportunities						

3. In thinking about overall "quality," please rate this school on each of the following characteristics:

	Extremely Important	Very Important	Important	Somewhat Important	Not at all Important	No Opinion
Helping students learn						
Understanding students' needs						
Understanding families' needs						
Accomplishing institutional goals						
Valuing its employees						
Communicating						
Continuously improving						
Building relationships						

4. If you were describing your child's experience at this school to a friend, what one word or phrase would best capture the essence of that experience?

5. In your own words, in what one area do you think this school could most improve?

Thank you for your participation!

CORE VALUES MATRIX

The Core Values Matrix plots what values resonate most across constituencies as a result of exercises in core values conducted in small groups. Close examination also reveals institutional alignments and misalignments.

Constituency	Board of Trustees	Administrative Leadership	Faculty and Staff	Students	Parent Leaders	Alumni	Other
Number of groups participating							
Number of individuals participating							
Top five most frequently mentioned values	1. 2. 3. 4. 5.	1. 2. 3. 4. 5.	1. 2. 3. 4. 5.	1. 2. 3. 4. 5.	1. 2. 3. 4. 5.	1. 2. 3. 4. 5.	1. 2. 3. 4. 5.

DEVELOPING A STATEMENT OF CORE VALUES

Directions

1. List the handful of core values that are most repeated across constituencies. These will be the values around which the campus community is most clearly aligned (see Core Values Matrix).

2. Develop a "Statement of Core Values" based on the ways these essential and enduring beliefs shape and drive your school's actions, outcomes, behaviors, decisions, relationships, and delivery of its mission.

Value	Value Statement 'We believe…', 'We value…', 'We stand for…', 'We are committed to…', 'We embrace…', 'We hold to…'

3. Apply the following tests for Core Values Statements:

1. Do these statements capture the essence of our school?

2. Do these statements describe us at our best?

3. Will these statements guide decision-making in the daily and long-term delivery of our school's mission?

4. Will these statements create and sustain alignment, especially in times of change?

5. Can these statements live with us indefinitely?

BRAINSTORMING A MISSION STATEMENT

When new work is done in articulating a school's core values, it is important to re-examine the school's mission statement for alignment with those values. This potentially arduous task can be readily simplified by using the following template suggested by authors Tom Justice and David Jamieson in their book, *The Facilitator's Fieldbook*, as a guide to answering the all-important questions around purpose and as a way to connect purpose to values.

Your strategic planning team should arrive at consensus on key content points by completing the prompts below. Then a small writing group can work the content into a clear and purposeful statement that answers the question "Why do we exist?" Ultimately, your board of trustees must accept any revisions recommended by the strategic planning team.

Believing that (critical values)

We exist to (primary purpose)

For (primary beneficiaries)

So that (key outcomes)

— *Adapted from Tom Justice and David W. Jamieson,* The Facilitator's Fieldbook *(American Management Association, 1999).*

MISSION STATEMENT REVIEW FOR EXCELLENCE AND CONGRUENCY WITH VALUES

Assign a mission review committee from the strategic planning team to consider your school's existing mission statement in light of the following test of excellence. If necessary, make revisions and present the revised statement to the board of trustees for approval.

Tests of Excellence for an Independent School Mission Statement

1. Does the mission statement answer the question "Why do we exist?"
2. Is it consistent with core values?
3. Is it clear, understandable, and memorable?
4. Will it endure?
5. Will it serve as a basis for operational as well as strategic decision-making?
6. Does it give all who see it or hear it a compelling reason to support your school?

Existing Mission Statement

Exemplary Mission Statement

STRATEGIC ISSUES MATRIX

Complete the following matrix by naming the top three strategic issues — those internal or external forces or factors that most significantly impact your school — identified by each constituency group through your research. Include results from peer reviews and STEEP (social, technological, environmental, economic, and political) factors.

Constituency Group or External Research Basis	Top Strategic Issue	Secondary Strategic Issue	Tertiary Strategic Issue
Board of Trustees			
Administration			
Faculty and Staff			
Students			
Parents			
Alumni			
Peer Reviews			
STEEP Factors			

APPRECIATIVE INQUIRY

"The major assumption of Appreciative Inquiry is that in every organization something works and change can be managed through the identification of what works and how to do more of what works."
— Sue Annis Hammond, *The Thin Book of Appreciative Inquiry*
  (second edition, Thin Book Publishing, 1998)

In her book, Hammond outlines David L. Cooperrider and Suresh Srivastva's 4-D AI model in the following steps, which have been adapted to an independent school setting.

1. *Discover* — Appreciate "The Best of What Is"

   Find examples of the *best of your school* by applying Appreciative Inquiry's Three Classic Questions:

   ■ Think back on your career at this school. Locate a moment that was a high point, when you felt most effective and engaged. Describe how you felt and what made the situation possible.
   ■ Without being humble, describe what you value most about yourself, your work, your school.
   ■ Determine what circumstances made the best possible.
   ■ Describe your three concrete wishes for the future of this school based on the best of what you have experienced.

2. *Dream* — Envision "What Might Be"

   Take the stories and envision what *might* be in your school. Write a "provocative proposition" applying "what if" to all the common themes. Then write affirmative present tense statements incorporating the common themes.

   > Example: *"What if* we reflected all the attributes of a community of learners?" becomes "We reflect all the attributes of a community of learners."

3. *Design* — Consent to "What Should Be"

   Determine the *changes in structure and process* that must occur to fulfill this vision.

4. *Destiny* — Experience "What Can Be"

   Implement the changes necessary to fulfill the vision.

DOES YOUR VISION HAVE IMPACT?

Powerful visions inspire bold actions that create high impact. Weak visions do not. Test your vision statement against the following criteria to gauge its impact power.

1. Write your draft vision.

2. Apply the following criteria to your draft vision to determine its potential to inspire and motivate action.

High-Impact Vision Criteria			
	Yes	No	Needs Improvement
1. It is a vivid description of a desired future that is a dramatic stretch from where the school is today.			
2. It is clear, understandable, and memorable.			
3. It inspires passion, compels action, and serves as a rallying call.			
4. It is consistent with school values and mission.			
5. It sets a clear direction and creates alignment in decision-making across the institution.			
6. When realized, it will resolve the school's strategic issues.			

"WHAT IF...?" SCENARIOS

"What if" scenarios suggest alternative ways to respond to critical issues and how various strategic choices might impact your school's future.

1. Develop a "What if...?" scenario based on the issues the school faces now and in the near term.

2. Discuss the scenario based on the following questions:
   - What does this future look like in detail?
   - What are the positives and negatives of this future scenario?
   - What do we think about this scenario? How do we feel about it?
   - What would cause this scenario to happen?

3. Brainstorm a list of possible outcomes of the scenario.
   - What if we do nothing?
   - What if we emphasize...?
   - What if we improve...?
   - What if...?

4. Arrive at consensus around what would be a satisfactory resolution three to five years from now of the question posed by the "what if" scenario. This is your vision of future success.

5. Develop a list of the four to six most significant actions you would have to take to achieve your vision. These are your goals.

6. Work your vision and goals into a three- to five-year plan using the template below.

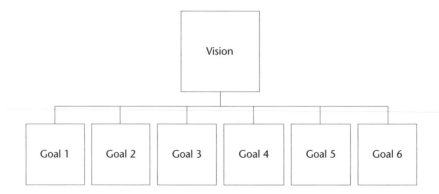

GOAL-SETTING USING GAP ANALYSIS

Resources
Core values, mission, and vision statements
Strategic issues
SWOT Analysis Results

Directions
Complete the following:

If this is what the school stands for (values)…

and this is our school's purpose (mission)…

and this is what we see as our idealized future (vision)…

Then these are the four to six things (goals) we must accomplish to bridge the gap between where we are today and where we want to be, including lists of resources we have and those we need to reach each goal…(complete the goal and resource blocks in the diagram).

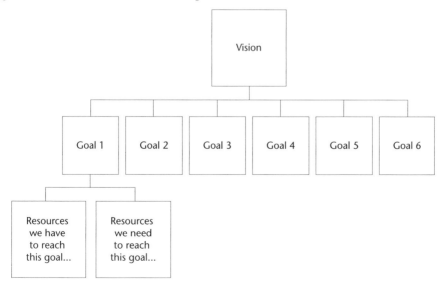

INITIATIVE DEVELOPMENT

Sponsor (Name the planning group proposing these initiatives)		
Goal (Identify which goal from the plan)		
Strategy (Identify which strategy under the goal)	**Initiative Description**	**Expected Outcomes** (List the top three expected outcomes for this initiative)

COST/NO COST VIEW OF INITIATIVES

#	Initiative Description	This Year			Next Year			Following Year		
		No Cost	Cost		No Cost	Cost		No Cost	Cost	
			Funded	Not Funded		Funded	Not Funded		Funded	Not Funded

DEFINING PERFORMANCE INDICATORS

In his book, *Measuring Performance* (Measurement International, 2000), Bob Frost writes that "Performance metrics are mostly derived from the strategy, mission, and goals of the organization, and factors important to key stakeholders." Dr. Frost's three-step method of defining performance indicators described below illustrates a simple yet definitive approach to deciding exactly what to measure and how:

Step 1. Identify what is crucial to the overall success of your business strategy (performance topic).

Step 2. Identify where and how you must succeed (critical success factors).

Step 3. Identify the evidence that each critical success factor has been reached (performance indicators).

Your school's strategic plan, whatever its organizational hierarchy, provides a natural context for creating performance metrics. Using it, you can identify the specific things you will watch as you track the success of your plan's goals, objectives, and/or initiatives.

Here is an adaptation of Frost's model in template form.

Performance Topic (Strategic plan goal, objective, initiative, or constituency)	Critical Success Factors Where must we succeed in this goal, objective, initiative, or with this constituency? How must we succeed in this goal, objective, initiative, or with this constituency?	Performance Indicators What are the measures of success?

STRATEGIC COMMUNICATION PLAN FOR STRATEGIC PLAN

Audience	Desired Outcome(s)	Communications Tool(s)	Method(s) or Venue(s)	Timeframe

BIBLIOGRAPHY

Allison, Michael, and Kaye, Jude, *Strategic Planning for Nonprofit Organizations* (John Wiley & Sons, 1997).*

Allison, Michael, and Kaye, Jude, *Strategic Planning for Nonprofit Organizations* (2nd edition, John Wiley & Sons, 2005).*

Burkhart, Patrick J., and Reuss, Suzanne, *Successful Strategic Planning: A Guide for Nonprofit Agencies and Organizations* (Sage Publications, 2002).

Bryson, John M., *Strategic Planning for Public and Nonprofit Organizations* (Jossey-Bass, 1995).

Bryson, John M., *Strategic Planning for Public and Nonprofit Organizations* (3rd edition, Jossey-Bass, 2004).

Carey, Stephen C., *The Association and Nonprofit Strategic Planning and Research Guide: A Workbook of Models, Templates and Best Practices for Creating Simple, Effective, Research-based Strategic Plans Tied to Operations for Volunteers and Staff* (AMMR Press, 2006). See the Guide at *www.ammr.com*.

Chait, Richard P., Ryan, William P., and Taylor, Barbara E., *Governance as Leadership: Reframing the Work of Nonprofit Boards* (John Wiley & Sons, 2004).

Collins, James C., "Aligning Actions and Values," *Leader to Leader* (Summer 1996).

Collins, James C., *Good to Great: Why Some Companies Make the Leap...and Others Don't* (HarperCollins, 2001).

Collins, James C. and Porras, Jerry I., *Built to Last: Successful Habits of Visionary Companies* (HarperCollins, 1994).

Drucker, Peter F., *Management: Tasks, Responsibilities, Practices* (Harper and Row, 1974).

Drucker, Peter F., *The Practice of Management* (reissued edition, HarperCollins, 1993).

Frost, Bob, *Crafting Strategy* (Measurement International, 2000).

Gladwell, Malcolm, *The Tipping Point* (Little, Brown and Company, 2000).

Hammond, Sue Annis, *The Thin Book of Appreciative Inquiry* (second edition, Thin Book Publishing, 1998).

Hesselbein, Frances, "Carry a Big Basket," *Leader to Leader* (Spring 2002).

Independent Schools: Preparing Students for Achievement in College and Beyond, (NAIS, 2004). Available at *www.nais.org*.

Justice, Tom, and Jamieson, David W., *The Facilitator's Fieldbook* (American Management Association, 1999).

Martinelli, Frank, *Strategic Planning Manual* (The Center for Public Skills Training, 1994).

Mintzberg, Henry, *The Rise and Fall of Strategic Planning* (Free Press, 1994).

Moore, Mark H., *Working Paper #18, The Public Value Scorecard: A Rejoinder and an Alternative to "Strategic Performance Measurement and Management in Non-Profit Organizations" by Robert Kaplan* (Hauser Center for Nonprofit Organizations at Harvard University, 2003).

NAIS Opinion Leaders Survey: Forecasting Independent Education to 2025, (NAIS, 2005). Available at *www.nais.org*.

* All quotes and materials cited are reprinted with permission of John Wiley & Sons, Inc.

Ogilvy, James, "What Strategists Can Learn from Sartre," *Strategy + Business* (Winter 2003).

Olsen, Howard W., and Olsen, Nancy D., *Strategic Planning Made Easy for Nonprofit Organizations* (M3 Planning, 2005).

Stone, Susan F., *Shaping Strategy,* (NAIS, 1993).

Schwartz, Peter, *Inevitable Surprises: Thinking Ahead in a Time of Turbulence* (Gotham, 2004).

The State of Independent School Governance: An NAIS Research Study, (NAIS, 2006). Available at *www.nais.org.*

Values Added: The Lifelong Returns of an Independent School Education, (NAIS, 2004). Available at *www.nais.org.*

Watkins, Jane Magruder, and Mohr, Bernard, *Appreciative Inquiry: Change at the Speed of Imagination* (Jossey-Bass, Pfeiffer, 2001).

www.nais.org.: Type in "Strategic Planning" in the Quick Search box on the NAIS front page to get other resources available from NAIS.

ABOUT THE AUTHORS AND CONTRIBUTORS

Bruce Butterfield, *President*
The Forbes Group, Vienna, VA

In his current position, Butterfield guides organizations through strategic thinking, planning, implementation, and organizational design, and conducts leadership research. He has developed national and global strategies to help several industries and professions adapt to the structural demands and market pressures of new technology. Butterfield has four decades of strategic management and public relations experience working primarily through the association sector in the United States, European Union, and Asia. He has served in executive capacities with seven national organizations in the food, housing, and insurance industries and the legal profession. Founder or cofounder of four national organizations, he has developed advocacy campaigns at the national and local level in the areas of public health, product safety, industry promotions, transportation, standards development, and professional certification and licensure. His education includes a bachelor of science degree from Iowa State University and postgraduate institutes at Yale, Syracuse, and New York University.

Christina Drouin, *Founder and Executive Director*
Center for Strategic Planning, Boca Raton, FL

As a strategy consultant and process facilitator, Drouin supports independent school trustees, heads, and administrative leadership teams in their commitment to building sustainable schools with local and global impact. She is known for her innovative work in adapting business models, principles, and practices to school settings and as a pioneer of social marketing in the 1980s. Over the past three decades, she has facilitated hundreds of strategic planning, strategic marketing, and change initiatives for health, education, and faith-based nonprofits. Drouin is a chapter author of NAIS's *Marketing Independent Schools in the 21st Century,* a CASE Circle of Excellence Gold Medal Award Winner, and an award-winning speaker at national independent school conferences. A former classroom teacher, she has also been an independent school administrator, served on nonprofit boards, and is a co-founder of *I Want to Learn English Language Labs,* a global educational nonprofit that brings English language learning to children in developing nations. Her education includes a bachelor of arts degree in English and secondary education from Framingham State College and postgraduate work at Boston University School of Public Communication.

Marc T. Frankel, *Senior Consultant and Partner*
Triangle Associates of St. Louis, MO

A psychologist by training, Dr. Frankel facilitates governance workshops, leadership development programs, and strategic planning in the United States and around the world. Among his accomplishments are the development of evaluation methodologies for governing boards and senior academic and administrative leaders, and co-founding the School Leadership Institute for the National Association of Independent Schools (NAIS). He has also written or co-written numerous articles and white papers on issues in governance and leadership. A former independent school trustee and a practicing psychologist, Dr. Frankel's professional training occurred at Emory University and the University of Missouri–Columbia.

Judith L. Schechtman, *Senior Consultant and Partner*
Triangle Associates of St. Louis, MO

With a wealth of experience coaching executives, physicians, nursing school faculty, and other professionals, Schechtman serves on the faculty for the NAIS School Leadership Program and the NAIS Institute for New Heads. An adjunct professor in the School of Social Work at Washington University in St. Louis, she teaches courses related to individual and family issues. Her clinical specialties include helping individuals deal effectively with trauma and life changes. She holds a master's degree in social work from Washington University, and her post-graduate training includes certificates from Masters and Johnson Institute and the International Critical Incident Stress Foundation.

Josh Stern, *Director of Administrative Programs*
St. Paul's Episcopal School, Oakland, CA

Before joining the St. Paul's administration, Stern was a sixth grade humanities teacher for four years. While a teacher, Stern served as a faculty member on the school's Strategic Planning Committee. He left St. Paul's to earn an M.A. degree in educational policy from Stanford University and returned to St. Paul's to serve in his current position. Annually, as co-chair of St. Paul's Strategic Planning Committee, Stern leads the board through the review of the strategic plan by reporting on the work to date, researching local market trends, and benchmarking data. That group is now updating the school's strategic plan. On a daily basis, Stern works with the administrative team to problem-solve operations as they relate to the school's expanded enrollment. He also serves as the project manager for the school's construction initiatives. For example, he has managed the completion of a seismic retrofit to the school's elementary school building and a renovation to the school's middle school building. He is also helping St. Paul's prepare for a second phase of the school's facilities upgrade.

Bruce B. Stewart, *Head of School*
Sidwell Friends School, Washington, DC
Since 1998, Stewart has headed Sidwell Friends. Born and raised in Massachusetts, he received an A.B. degree in economics from Guilford College and a master's of education degree from the University of North Carolina. His professional career began as dean of student affairs at North Carolina School for the Arts. He then moved to Guilford College serving as director of admissions, followed by assistant to the president, then acting academic dean, and, finally, provost of the college. In 1984, he relocated to Pennsylvania to be head of Abington Friends School for 14 years before moving to Sidwell Friends. Stewart serves as the chair of the board of School Year Abroad and on the boards of NAIS, Bullis School, Friends Council on Education, and Guilford College.

Lawrence S. Sykoff, *Head of School*
Ranney School, Tinton Falls, NJ
Sykoff has been the head at Ranney School since 1993. He also serves on the regional advisory board for the American Cancer Society and is co-chair of the Business and Industry Council for the Society. In addition, he is on the board of directors of the Count Basie Theater Foundation and the board of the Monmouth University School of Communications. He has previously been a member of the finance committee of the New Jersey Association of Independent Schools, and chair of its Marketing and Development Committee. He has received the Congressional Service Award from Congressman Frank Pallone and was recently featured in the University of San Diego Dean's Report as a distinguished leader and an outstanding alumnus who has made a difference in the field of education. He holds a B.B.A. from the City University of New York, an M. Ed. from the University of San Diego in educational psychology, and Ed.D. from the University of San Diego in educational leadership and organizational management.

INDEX